THE ENDLESS FAIRWAY

The Golfer's Guide To
THE CAROLINAS
Including Georgia's Golden Isles

BRETT BORTON & THE EDITORS OF
LINKS MAGAZINE

A Fireside Book • Published by Simon & Schuster
New York London Toronto Sydney Tokyo Singapore

FIRESIDE
Rockefeller Center
1230 Avenue of the Americas
New York, New York 10020

Principal photographer—Mike Klemme/Golfoto
Supervising editor: Brett Borton, Mark Brown,
James Max Lane
Designed by James Max Lane

Manufactured in the United States of America

3   5   7   9   10   8   6   4   2

Library of Congress Cataloging-in-Publication Data

Borton, Brett.
The endless fairway : the golfer's guide to the Carolinas,
including Georgia's Golden Isles / Brett Borton & the editors
of Links Magazine.
        p.   cm.
        "A Fireside book."
  1. Golf courses—North Carolina—Directories.   2. Golf
courses—South Carolina—Directories.   3. Golf courses—
Georgia—Golden Isles—Directories.   4. Golf resorts—North
Carolina—Directories.   5. Golf resorts—South Carolina—
Directories.   6. Golf resorts—Georgia—Golden Isles—
Directories.   I. Southern links (Hilton Head Island, S.C.)
II. Title.   III. Title: Golfer's guide to the Carolinas, including
Georgia's Golden Isles.
        GV982.N8B67   1991
796.352'06'8756—dc20   93-48784
                                                      CIP
ISBN 0-671-74335-X

Table of Contents

Author's Note

The author wishes to thank the following people and organizations, without whom the successful completion of this book would not have been possible: all the marketing and public relations directors of the properties described herein for their gracious support and assistance; Mike Klemme of Golfoto for another round of superb photography; Max Lane, Cindy Spaulding and everyone at LINKS magazine for their usual stellar performances on this project; Tim Hays, once again, for helping to give birth to *The Endless Fairway* series and Jeff Neuman of Simon & Schuster for believing in it; my mother and father, Arthur and Betty Borton, for introducing me to golf in the Carolinas at an early age; and my wife Sara and son Jarrett, for their unwavering love and support. Finally, this book is dedicated in loving memory to my laughing moonbeam, Haley Ann Carpenter Borton.

—Brett Borton

Editor's Note

As this is the fourth and (to date) final volume in *The Endless Fairway* series, let me add thanks to LINKS photographers Mike Klemme, Chris Duthie, and Mark Brown for the pictures; to Ed Cherry, Brett Borton, George Fuller, and Ray March for the words; to Randy Guyton and Ann Lane for their editing and proofing; to Cindy Spaulding for acquiring the photography; to Kitty Bartell for supervising the photo separations; and to Stu Gottesman and Jeff Neuman at Simon & Schuster for steering the project through to the end. It's been a great ride!

—James M. Lane

How to Use this Book

FIRST OF ALL
The Endless Fairway is organized by chapters covering major golf "pockets." Each chapter includes a summary of all public courses, plus sections on area Attractions, Popular Dining Options, non-golf Activities, and an introduction to the region. The book also provides an in-depth look at the chief golf resorts. "Also in the Area" highlights public courses which do not have resort accommodations or amenities. The book does not cover private or par-3 courses.

INDEXES
In addition to the course index which begins on page 189, we have provided a Resort Index, beginning on page 180, which lists all the major hotels and villa complexes at the resorts covered in the book, with rates (as of November, 1993), telephone numbers, and a summary of amenities (including non-golf activities).

GREENS FEES
Greens fees are quoted at the peak season rate, including cart. To simplify matters, we use the following formula:

Low	$0-$25
Moderate	$26-$50
High	$51-$75
Very High	More than $75

Look for discounts during the off-season and at off-peak times of the day. Many courses offer discounts of $10-$22 if you do not require a cart.

COURSE RECOMMENDATIONS
Courses which have special merit are marked with a single asterisk (*). Certain outstanding courses are marked with a double asterisk (**). Naturally, these evaluations only represent the judgement of the editors.

COURSE AND SLOPE RATINGS
Each chapter summary includes latest available USGA course and slope ratings for the regular men's and women's (or forward) tees.

Introduction

Ask a group of golf historians when and where this country's version of the game began, and you'll more than likely get several different responses. So for the sake of argument—and as a seemingly suitable introduction to golf in the Carolinas and Georgia's barrier islands—allow me to set the record straight. The fact is, while the first modern-era golf club in the U.S. was founded in Yonkers, NY, in 1888, there is documented evidence that golf as we know it—or some semblance thereof—was played as early as the mid-1700s in the Carolina and Georgia Lowcountry.

Noted author, columnist and golf historian Charles Price, among others, is a leading proponent of this claim. Several years ago, Price unearthed documentation confirming the formation of the South Carolina Golf Club in 1786, making it the oldest organized golf club in the U.S. Membership was comprised of transplanted Scottish and English merchants—still somewhat loyal to the customs of the Mother country after the Revolution —who played on park land in Charleston known as Harleston's Green.

There is also evidence that British merchants in Savannah, Ga., 100 miles to the south of Charleston, formed a golf club of sorts as early as 1796. Meetings were held regularly and included the business of "drawing for finders," or choosing forecaddies who would direct the golfers to the hole (there were no flagsticks in those days, or greens, for that matter). All of this is outlined in *The Carolina Lowcountry: Birthplace of American*

Golf, a 1980 book written by Price and George C. Rogers, Jr., Ph.D, a history professor at the University of South Carolina, and later substantiated by Terry Bunton in his 1989 book, *The History of the Heritage, 1969-1989.* As Bunton notes, the South Carolina Golf Club was re-chartered to the Harbour Town Golf Links on Hilton Head Island in 1969 as part of the inauguration of the Heritage Classic PGA tournament, today known as the MCI Heritage Classic.

The point of all this, other than to fan the flame of some spirited 19th hole debates, is to offer suitable grounds for the rich history of golf in the Carolinas and coastal Georgia.

What springs to mind at the mention of Carolina golf? Is it the glorious tradition of Pinehurst, the storied excellence of Hilton Head Island, or the unparalleled popularity of the Myrtle Beach "Grand Strand?" It's actually all of this, and much more. The Blue Ridge Mountain region of Western North Carolina, for instance, boasts some magnificent courses created in the 1920s by Donald Ross, who frequently migrated to the High Country from the sandhills of Pinehurst. Then there's Charleston—where it all began—and its concentration of outstanding courses that drew international attention during the 1991 Ryder Cup at Kiawah Island's Ocean Course.

And lest we forget about the Golden Isles, that strip of barrier islands off the Southeastern coast of Georgia. Golf has played a major role since the turn of the century on this playground of the elite; the Rockefellers, Morgans and Vanderbilts hacked along the windswept dunes of Jekyll Island as early as 1898, and Ohio automaker Howard Coffin made golf a part of the amenities at his Sea Island retreat, The Cloister, in the late 1920s. Bobby Jones, the former course-record holder on the Sea Island Golf Club's Plantation Nine, once called the course "one of the very best nines I have ever seen."

If nothing else, *"The Endless Fairway: The Golfer's Guide To The Carolinas and Georgia's Golden Isles"* is a celebration of the region and its grand golfing traditions. From the mountains to the Lowcountry, there is something here for everyone: world-ranked courses and hidden gems, luxurious accommodations and rustic retreats, bustling resorts and secluded hideaways.

Those of you who have been to the Carolinas are fully aware of the region's broad appeal. Those of us fortunate enough to live here welcome you to come stay and play in "God's Country," the birthplace of American golf. Hey, we may be arrogant, but at least we're not selfish.

Brett A. Borton
Hilton Head Island, SC, October, 1993

Lake Toxaway Golf Club, showing its brilliant fall coloring.

THE
MOUNTAINS

IMAGINE A PLACE WHERE COMMERCIAL DEVELOPMENT HAS BEEN largely overshadowed by vast acres of virgin wilderness. Where rolling foothills effortlessly blend into towering snow-capped peaks. Where people still craft by hand. Where storytelling is an art form, and music comes from the strings of banjos, fiddles and dulcimers in ballads such as "I'll Be Glad When You're Dead, You Rascal, You" or "A Woman's Tongue Will Never Take A Rest." Where row after row of Fraser firs stand majestically and offer the unmistakable scent of Christmas, even in

Reem's Creek is one of two American courses (the other is nearby Mount Mitchell) designed by the English master architect Fred Hawtree. The Hawtree firm, among other courses, designed Royal Birkdale in England, one of the host courses for the British Open. Pictured here is the par-3 17th.

July. Where city lights are muted by the spectacular panorama of a mountain sunset.

It is the Blue Ridge Mountain region of Western North Carolina, and while it may not be heaven, it's as close as you'll find anywhere east of the Mississippi. More than one resident has referred to the area as "God's

The Mountains

The Complete List of Courses Open to the Public

Location	Course	Address
Asheville	Great Smokies Hilton G.C.	1 Hilton Dr.
	*Grove Park Inn & C.C.	Country Club Rd.
Banner Elk	Beech Mountain	30 Pine Ridge Rd.
Black Mountain	Black Mountain G.C.	General Delivery
Blowing Rock	Hounds Ears Lodge & C.C.	Highway 105
Boone	Boone G.C.	Fairway Dr.
Burnsville	**Mount Mitchell G.C.	7590 Highway 80 S.
Canton	Springdale G.C.	Route 2, Box 271
Cashiers	*High Hampton Inn & C.C.	Highway 107 S.
Etowah	*Etowah Valley C.C. (27)	Brickyard Rd.
Flat Rock	*Kenmure G.C.	100 Clubhouse Dr.
	Lost Diamond Valley G.C. (9)	111 Highland Lake Rd.
Franklin	*Mill Creek Club	Route 1, Box 848
Hayesville	*Mountain Harbor G.C.	100 Mountain Harbor Dr.
Hendersonville	Crooked Creek G.C.	764 Crooked Creek Rd.
	*Cummings Cove G.C.	3000 Cummings Rd.
Lake Lure	Fairfield Mountain Resort—	
	*Apple Valley Course	201 Mountain Blvd.
	Bald Mountain Course	201 Mountain Blvd.
Lake Toxaway	*Lake Toxaway G.C.	P.O. Box 70
Linville	**Linville G.C.	P.O. Box 98
	**Linville Ridge G.& C.C.	P.O. Box 2270
Maggie Valley	*Maggie Valley C.C.	Country Club Dr.
Murphy	*Cherokee Hills G. & C.C.	Harshaw Rd.
Roaring Gap	High Meadows G. & C.C.	355 Country Club Dr.
Sapphire	Holly Forest C.C.	4000 Highway 64 W.
Seven Devils	Hanging Rock G.C.	1608 Skyland Dr.
Spruce Pine	Grassy Creek C.C.	101 Golf Course Rd.
Tryon	Red Fox C.C.	2 Club Rd.
Waynesville	**Laurel Ridge C.C.	630 Eagle Nest Rd.
	**Reem's Creek G.C.	Pink Fox Cove Rd.
	*Waynesville C.C. (27)	P.O. Box 390

* Recommended Course ** Highly Recommended

Country," and for good reason. From Maggie Valley to the High Country of Boone and Blowing Rock, this is a land of awe-inspiring scenery, endless activity, and folks who are just genuinely nice.

While people have made their homes in North Carolina's Blue Ridge Mountains since the first push westward, it is nature that continues to

Rating/Slope: Men	Women	Par	Cost	Phone
Executive	Executive	70	Low	(704) 253-5874
69.4/114	69.7/111	72	Moderate	(704) 252-2711
67.9/123	67.3/113	72	n/a	(704) 387-4717
66.9/113	68.1/109	71	Low	(704) 669-2710
67.9/108	66.8/110	72	n/a	(704) 963-5831
67.4/112	69.1/113	71	Moderate	(704) 264-8710
67.5/116	69.0/117	72	Moderate	(704) 675-5454
70.7/121	72.2/121	72	n/a	(704) 235-8451
—	—	71	Moderate	(704) 743-2411
72.5/124	72.5/117	72	Moderate	(704) 891-7141
69.1/125	70.2/123	72	Moderate	(704) 697-1200
Executive	Executive	36	Low	(704) 692-0143
68.5/113	66.4/113	72	Low	(704) 524-4653
69.1/119	64.8/108	72	n/a	(800) 462-4607
69.2/122	67.2/107	72	Low	(704) 692-2011
68.8/113	70.2/113	70	Moderate	(704) 891-7428
69.7/126	65.9/112	72	Moderate	(704) 625-9111
68.9/121	66.2/112	72	Moderate	(704) 625-9111
68.0/116	68.4/115	72	n/a	(704) 966-4661
70.4/129	69.3/119	72	n/a	(704) 733-4363
69.9/123	68.9/119	72	n/a	(704) 898-9741
68.9/118	69.8/117	71	Moderate	(704) 926-1616
70.0/113	68.0/107	72	Low	(704) 837-5853
69.8/118	66.6/106	72	Moderate	(919) 363-2445
67.0/118	66.8/112	70	Moderate	(704) 743-3441
67.0/110	66.5/110	72	Moderate	(704) 963-6565
68.1/116	67.5/109	72	Low	(704) 765-7436
70.8/124	70.4/118	72	Moderate	(704) 874-8251
68.7/118	67.7/113	72	Moderate	(704) 456-3200
70.1/127	66.9/114	72	Moderate	(704) 645-4393
64.8/100	67.0/104	70	Moderate	(704) 452-4617

endure here. The peaks and valleys of Western North Carolina now offer an array of resorts and other attractions, but they have only seemed to enhance what was here in the beginning. Wildlife still flourishes, streams are still crystal clear, and forests of birch, poplar, beech, hickory and oak are still undisturbed. This is one of those rare places where civilization has had the foresight to protect nature as well as enjoy it.

The cultural hub of Western North Carolina is Asheville, a city dominated by eclectic architecture and breathtaking natural beauty, where fiddlers and cloggers are as revered as some of the town's most famous residents (George W. Vanderbilt, whose grandfather built the magnificent Biltmore Estate, as well as great literary figures such as Thomas Wolfe and Carl Sandburg). Among cities comparable in size, Asheville is one of the country's best places to live. Having grown from a tiny trading village at the confluence of the French Broad and Swannanoa rivers, it has also become a major year-round resort city and remains one of the state's most popular travel destinations.

The mountains are most popular in the summer months. This is when the region can best display its magnificent outdoor treasures, not the least of which are its lush and rolling golf courses. These courses are rich in beauty, challenge and, in many cases, historical significance. In addition to the work of Donald Ross—the legendary Scotsman who moonlighted to the mountains when not overseeing Pinehurst's golf operations around the turn of the century—the mountains include two courses built by the oldest golf-course architecture firm in the world; two courses built by descendants of Frank Maples, the Pinehurst course superintendent who worked at Ross' side; and one course that's the offspring of a miniature links built for the enjoyment of the Rockefellers, Fords, Vanderbilts and Firestones.

Among them you can find difficult golf and easy golf. You can find rustic retreats and luxurious hotels. You can find few amenities outside of

golf, and you can find so much else to do that you might forget about golf. Such is the magic, and the majesty, of the North Carolina mountains.

The brilliant fall colors make September and October prime season for many veterans of Carolina mountain golf. Pictured here is the 15th hole at Mount Mitchell Golf Club. Designer Fred Hawtree filtered American course design principles through his English sensibility to create this broad, sweeping classic among mountain courses.

Getting There

The closest major airport is in Asheville, which is serviced by American Airlines and its regional commuter, American Eagle, as well as Delta and USAir. All major rental car companies are represented. By car, Interstate 40 passes through Asheville from the east and west; I-26 runs southeast all the way to Charleston, S.C.; U.S. 23/19A runs north and west; and I-240 is a perimeter route circumventing the city.

Weather

While most of the major resorts in the area are open year-round, the best time to visit is from late spring to early fall. High temperatures can reach into the mid-80s in the summer, but conditions are cooled dramatically by the mountain breezes. Winter brings temperatures in the 30s and 40s and heavy snowfall in the higher elevations. While skiiers delight in the many slopes found in the High Country around Banner Elk and Blowing Rock, getting there is not always so easy. Much of this section of the Blue Ridge Parkway is closed during the winter, and traveling on the smaller mountain roads can be hazardous in wintery conditions.

Far left: The highly rated Hounds Ears Resort is home to a short, attractive course that is built for scoring. Pictured here, the third hole.
Near left: Rolling hills, the signature of most of the mountain courses, are in splendid evidence at the second hole at Reem's Creek.

Activities

A drive along the Blue Ridge Parkway alone may be worth a visit to this region. Plan to do as much stopping and looking (and photographing) as driving; the highway is renowned for its scenic overlooks, recreation areas, trails, campgrounds, picnic areas, and roadside markers. But don't rush through it. Two or three days are ideal for traversing the entire route from Tennessee to Virginia. Besides, the speed limit is 45 miles per hour. Other outdoor activities center around the streams, brooks and rivers that lace the region. These waterways are a haven for anglers (check local regulations with regard to licensing before wetting a line), a roadway for horseback riders, and a crossroads for hikers exploring the magnificent trails that run through the mountains. Most notable is the Appalachian Trail, which runs along the crest of the state's highest mountains.

Attractions

When visiting in or around Asheville, the 12,000-acre Biltmore Estate is not to be missed. The highlight is the 250-room Biltmore House, a grand

European chateau built in the 19th century by the grandson of tycoon George Vanderbilt and furnished with prized antiques and art. Adjacent is the Biltmore Village, a series of restored English-style houses with a variety of shops and galleries. Five miles east of Asheville is the Folk Art Center, a contemporary wood-and-stone structure that features the finest in both traditional and contemporary handcrafts. Twenty-five miles southeast is Chimney Rock Park, featuring a granite monolith rising to a height of 315 feet with an observation lounge, a plethora of scenic trails, and picnic areas. A few miles further is Flat Rock, which is perhaps best known as the longtime home of poet Carl Sandburg. Sandburg's home and farm are preserved just as they were during his lifetime, and visitors are free to stroll around the grounds. Other area attractions include the Old Depot at Black Mountain (eight miles east of town), where local artisans work their trade and musicians frequently sing traditional ballads of the hills; and Ghost Town in the Sky in Maggie Valley (a few miles

Left: The High Hampton golf Club is routed through some of the most spectacular scenery in the mountains. Above: Ample tee times, a long and demanding course, and superb conditioning including bentgrass greens have put Etowah Valley at the top of the list for the serious golfer. Pictured here is the first hole on the West nine.

west of Asheville), a family entertainment center with recreated Western, mining and mountaineer towns, gunfights, saloons, and all sorts of characters milling about. You reach it by riding inclined railways or chair lifts - another treat for the kids. It's open from May through October only. In the "High Country" (Boone/Banner Elk/Blowing Rock areas), performances of "Horn in the West" are given nightly except Monday during the summer and depict the efforts of Daniel Boone to win the friendship of the native Cherokee Indians. In the town of Cherokee, located 48 miles southwest of Asheville, the Museum of the Cherokee Indians offers a fascinating look at the tribe's history and culture, and "Unto These Hills" is a powerful and moving live drama on the history of the Cherokee people. The show is presented at the outdoor Mountainside Theatre nightly except Sunday from mid-June through late August.

Shopping

The best shopping in the region is for antiques (country and English), local crafts, art, needlework, apparel, toys, gourmet foods and homemade mountain goodies. The Downtown Asheville Historic District offers more than 100 retail shops, and the smaller towns such as Maggie Valley, Cashiers, Black Mountain, Linville and Banner Elk offer more quaint, intimate shops with everything from homespun to luxury goods.

For More Information

The North Carolina Division of Travel & Tourism, Department of Economic and Community Development, 430 North Salisbury St., Raleigh, NC 27611, (800) VISIT NC, or (919) 733-4171, or the Asheville Convention & Visitors Bureau, P.O. Box 1010, Asheville, NC 28802, (800) 257-1300 or (704) 258-6111.

Popular Dining Options

Asheville: *The Market Place*, innovative veal, chicken and beef dishes made with fresh ingredients, offered by a knowledgeable and attentive staff in a relaxed atmosphere—don't forget the award-winning wine list; *Steven's Restaurant*, a Victorianesque dining room featuring International cuisine and specializing in rack of lamb, informally elegant; the *Grove Park Inn*, the city's grand old hotel where Sunday brunch is an Asheville tradition and the Friday night seafood buffet is equally popular; also featuring elegant gourmet dining in *Horizons Restaurant* and casual meals overlooking the mountains in the *Carolina Cafe*; and *Bill Stanley's Barbeque and Blue Grass*, a rustic, foot-stompin' local haunt with mouth-watering barbeque served in massive portions as well as smoked catfish, chicken and ham; stick around for the free-spirited mountain music and clogging that takes place just about every night except Sunday.

THE RESORTS IN DEPTH

The Blue Ridge Resorts
"A Golf Odyssey—Exploring Peak Season Across The Great Smoky Mountains"

About the same time Scotsman Thomas Mathison completed his trilogy "The Golf" some 200 years ago (current market value: $75,000, give or take a stroke), Daniel Boone and a handful of axmen cut a road running through the barrier of the Appalachian Mountains in Western North Carolina. Today, the Blue Ridge Parkway (market value: $124 million) covers 469 miles, 76,427.34 acres and has witnessed 400 million people rolling along its asphalt.

What has one to do with the other?

What was cleverly promoted at its inception in 1934 by President Franklin D. Roosevelt as a link between two national parks (the Great Smoky Mountains in North Carolina and the Shenandoah in Virginia) and an economic boost of tourists and jobs to the surrounding communities, the Blue Ridge Parkway, in truth, is a scenic golfway that puts travelers within a driver/9-iron of some of the South's finest golf.

From its lower apex off U.S. 441 just 19 miles south of the Tennessee border near Cherokee, to its merge near Charlottesville with the George Washington Skyline Drive, the Parkway broaches dozens of wonderful golf courses that bloom with dogwoods and rhododendrons in the spring, are naturally air-conditioned in the summer, and are awash with red, orange and yellow in the fall.

When your ship comes in, when you have nothing to do for a couple of months but travel and play golf, you might try this golfing pilgrimage that begins in the hills of Tennessee, near the Parkway's western beginning, continues through the Asheville and High Country areas and concludes at a slopeside course (Wintergreen) in Virginia. At no point will you venture more than an hour's detour from the Parkway. Most stops, in fact, are only minutes away.

The "golfway" first begins to pick up a head of steam in Haywood County, one of Western North Carolina's golf hubs. Maggie Valley Resort and Waynesville Country Club Inn, two of the region's most popular resorts, flourish in the summer but are also open year-round.

Maggie Valley Resort has long been regarded as offering one of Western North Carolina's best golf courses; it has hosted several N.C. Opens and always has excellent bentgrass greens. The front nine is relatively flat and open; the back nine is hilly and rises 900 feet by the time you reach the stiff, uphill 13th (a 398-yard par-4). What Maggie takes on those holes, she gives back on the downhill 17th, a short par-4 of 293 yards from an elevated tee, and the par-5 18th, which rolls down toward the clubhouse while hopping a stream twice.

Located 35 miles west of Asheville, Maggie's accommodations include lodge rooms and one- and two-bedroom villas, and its other amenities include a heated pool, tennis courts a restaurant with scenic mountain views, and a lounge with nightly entertainment.

Waynesville Country Club figured out in the 1920s that thousands of lowlanders found the mountains the perfect tonic for insect-generated disease and general heat-induced malaise and constructed an inn and golf course to accommodate them. The club is still thriving and has grown

The 14th hole at Mount Mitchell, with its forgiving catchment bunker near the water and a wide-open entrance to the green allowing either the run-in or the lofted approach.

The 12th hole at Maggie Valley is the third in a four hole stretch on the back nine that rises 900 feet in elevation. Maggie Valley has hosted several North Carolina Opens over the years.

with the times with nine new holes, meeting facilities, and cottages and villas. The shortish golf course (the original layout measures 6,080 yards) is a favorite of average and senior players, and requires no forced carries over water.

Many come here, however, for the food and the entertainment. Waynesville Country Club is renowned for its beef, its fresh baked breads and homemade desserts, and its Saturday night buffets. There's clogging on Fridays and dance bands on Saturdays - on the terrace, weather permitting. Conference facilities handle groups of up to 200.

Within 25 miles of each other, and just a short drive from the Parkway's southernmost tangent at Beech Gap, are High Hampton Inn & Country Club, and Greystone Inn/Lake Toxaway Country Club.

High Hampton Inn & Country Club, originally the estate of Confederate General Wade Hampton, is located off U.S. 64 in Cashiers and has been called the "ultimate family summer camp." Generations have returned over its 70-year existence for summertime R&R that includes golf, tennis, skeet and trap shooting, bass and trout fishing in more than 40 acres of lakes, swimming, horseback riding, boating, archery and hiking.

If you're looking for luxury, keep away from High Hampton. If you want character (it's listed on the National Register of Historic Places), night-time sweaters, good food and no worries, the door is always open. The architecture of the Inn and guest cottages is rustic and blends with the natural beauty of the mountains and valley. In the lobby of the Inn, a huge stone chimney with its four fireplaces provides guests a warm and friendly welcome. Guest rooms have walls of sawmill-finished pine, are furnished with comfortable mountain-crafted furniture, and are "naturally" cooled (translation: no air conditioning, but none is needed). The menu at High Hampton features American cuisine with fresh vegetables and herbs from the Inn's garden and homemade baked goods. Inn rooms come on the American Plan (three meals daily), while the resort's limited number of rental homes are available on either the American or European Plan (no meals).

High Hampton's par-71 George Cobb golf course gently rolls just over 6,000 yards with beautiful mountain views and has only one bunker - and that's for the purposes of Mason and Bonnie Rudolph's annual golf schools.

The Greystone Inn is about 15 miles east just off Highway 64 in Lake Toxaway and, with neighboring **Lake Toxaway Country Club**, offers an elegant turnkey summertime recluse. Recreation at the Inn includes skiing, sailing, canoeing, tennis, croquet and bocci. For the less active there's afternoon tea, twilight boat cruises, and impromptu singalongs around the Inn's baby grand piano. The Greystone is also on the National Register of Historic Places (it was originally built in 1915 as a private residence), and is the state's only Four Diamond country inn, as recognized by the American Automobile Association.

The Greystone has 33 rooms with an engaging mix of antique furnishings and modern comforts (including Jacuzzis in all the rooms). Many rooms have their own working fireplaces. A stone fireplace is also the focal point in the oak-paneled living room; the library is a beautifully appointed oasis; and the terrace is the perfect setting for cocktails. In addition to the main house guest rooms, there are six very nice two-and three-bedroom cottages that come equipped with full kitchens.

Lake Toxaway Country Club opened in 1963 with a solid back nine, but a front nine with several overly short holes and a measurement from the tips of only 2,652 yards. Thus, The Lake Toxaway Company—owner and manager of the lake, the Inn, the golf course and the surrounding real estate development—retained longtime Joe Lee associate Rocky Roquemore to supervise the renovation of the golf course to bring it up to championship caliber. All of the greens on the course have been rebuilt, two new holes have been added, one discarded, and two others combined into one. The changes make the course a challenge commensurate with the surrounding beauty.

Waynesville Country Club. The routing of Waynesville was created in 1924 by Donald Ross, although he left the actual work of building the course to John Drake. Small wonder, since in 1923-24 Ross also completed Oakland Hills, Bannockburn, Cape Fear, Linville G.C., River Oaks in Houston, as well as both courses at Oak Hill in Rochester, site of the 1995 Ryder Cup Matches.

Located eight miles west of Hendersonville on U.S. 64 is **Etowah Valley Country Club & Golf Lodge**. Known since its opening in the 1960s as perhaps the area's top all-around golf course (i.e., condition and challenge to competent golfers), Etowah has moved the last decade to accommodate traveling golfers with abundant new facilities.

There are 27 holes of golf; the original 18—consisting of the South and West nines—is a long, demanding course of 7,108 yards with several difficult par-4s. The newer nine, the North course, is a par-37 of 3,404 yards. All three courses have bentgrass throughout. Since the lodge only accommodates 70 guests at a time, ample tee times and privacy are rarely a concern. There's also an excellent practice facility as well as a lighted putting green outside the lodge.

Other amenities at Etowah Valley include a bentgrass croquet green that the U.S. Croquet Association named "the best new croquet club in America" for 1991. The meal plan at the lodge includes a full country breakfast and a four-course dinner.

From here you can make a northern detour from the Parkway through Asheville, home to two of the most popular hotel-and-golf properties— **Grove Park Inn and Country Club** and the **Great Smokies Hilton**. The Grove Park Inn offers mountain vacationing that is rustic and at the same time luxurious. A favorite haunt of the Southern elite since 1913, it has hosted such notables as F. Scott Fitzgerald, FDR, Woodrow Wilson, Thomas Edison and Henry Ford, and is listed on the National Register of Historic Places. The Inn is built on the side of Sunset Mountain at an elevation of 3,100 feet. In its "great hall" lobby, flanked on each end by 14-foot fireplaces, comfortably padded chairs and sofas create a feeling of coziness despite the expansive 120-foot dimensions of the room.

Donald Ross designed the Grove Park Inn Country Club, a scenic mountain course that plays 6,172 yards to a par of 71. Other diversions include nine tennis courts, indoor and outdoor swimming pools, a shopping arcade, several fine restaurants, and three lounges.

The Great Smokies Hilton, in addition to offering high-quality guest rooms (some with wet bars) in the Hilton tradition, features a heated pool, sauna, tennis, an excellent dining room, and an 18-hole golf course. This is a short (5,111) but tight layout with tree-lined fairways and a winding stream that comes into play at some point or another on every hole.

Just north of the city awaits a pair of unparalleled golf experiences. Three generations of the Hawtree family of Oxford, England, have designed more than 250 golf courses over the past century, and the only two they've ever done in the United States are near Asheville. Developers Jim Floyd—his father was a writer for the old *Golfdom* magazine—and Lee King hired Fred Hawtree to design their **Mount Mitchell Golf Club** in the early 1970s. And when they added **Reem's Creek Golf Club** in 1989, they went back to the Hawtrees. Fred had gone into semi-retirement, leaving son Martin to handle most of the Reem's Creek job.

Mount Mitchell is located near Burnsville, N.C., about 45 minutes north of Asheville. The 6,475-yard course sits in a valley more than 3,000 feet beneath the highest peak in the Eastern U.S. (Mount Mitchell, at 6,684 feet). The terrain the course is routed through is relatively tame for such heights, but golfers at every turn are distracted by the views and

The 10th hole at Hounds Ears. George Cobb, the architect of Hounds Ears, also served as design consultant to Augusta National in the 1950s and 1960s.

challenged by Hawtree's use of the natural streams and forests to define the course. Accommodations are available on-site in Albert's Golf Lodge as well as in private villas and homes.

Reem's Creek is 12 miles north of Asheville and is the first public course of championship caliber to open in Buncombe County in decades. The younger Hawtree constructed a fairly short course (6,464 yards from the tips) that draws more on a golfer's patience, smarts and aim than it does his strength. There are several holes with blind tee shots and several others that require lay-up shots off the tee.

Both Mount Mitchell and Reem's Creek fill a nice niche in the hills in that neither is a pure resort course (thus monopolized by guests) nor a private club (thus closed to the public). Both are good tests of golf, and visitors constantly rave over the conditions. Both courses feature bentgrass greens and fairways (which are manicured like greens), and the grounds crews insist on walk-mowing the greens rather than compacting the surfaces with heavy machinery.

Our Blue Ridge golf odyssey leaves North Carolina with two of the finest resorts in the High Country: **Hound Ears Club** and **Linville Golf Club/Esceeola Lodge.**

Hound Ears is regarded by regulars as a fun golf course, one easy enough that if you normally shoot 85, you'll shoot 81 there and possibly into the 70s. But it's tight enough, and there are enough hazards (Watauga River meanders as a stream and pond on 17 holes). It's always in immaculate condition and one of George Cobb's best works. Accommodations at Hound Ears are plush, and guests are treated quite well (forget your umbrella?...The Hound Ears staff will put one outside your door on questionable days). Rooms and suites are luxurious, the setting is gorgeous, and the grounds are beautifully landscaped. The lodge is open year-round, and its other amenities include a swimming pool, tennis, fishing, and, in the winter months, skiing.

Together, Esceeola Lodge and Linville Golf Club are historical experiences. The Lodge was built in 1926, and it is on the National Register of Historic Places. It is also rates Four Stars from Mobil and a Silver Medal from *Golf* magazine.

Donald Ross ventured into the High Country from his Pinehurst home in 1929 to design Linville Golf Club, which stands today as a course held dearly to the hearts of visitors and members. It is classic Ross with plenty of elevated, mounded greens and demanding long-iron shots. With no bulldozers around in those days, Ross cleared some fairways beneath Grandfather Mountain and let nature do the rest.

The scenery is rich. A neat row of cottages line the fairways of the first and second holes. A creek meanders in front of the green of the difficult 449-yard, par-4 third hole. A lake borders the green of the par-5 fourth hole. And several cart paths disappear into thick foliage and greenery before sprouting back into the sunshine.

The lodge staff takes care of breakfast and dinner, and sandwiches are available at the golf shop for lunch. The resort does offer tennis, fishing and swimming, and there's a parlor for cards and general horseplay in the evening. Most groups at Esceeola Lodge, however, retire early so to not let anything stand in the way of 36 holes the following day.

Where mountain golf is concerned, early to bed and early to rise never made more sense.

ALSO IN THE AREA

Beech Mountain G.C., Banner Elk
Hilly course with narrow fairways and small greens. Accommodations include three mountaintop inns and chalet rentals nearby.

Black Mountain G.C., Black Mountain
Features the world's longest par-6 at 747 yards. Open year-round.

Blue Mountain C.C., Mars Hill
Challenging mountain course with beautiful views and elevations up to
4,875 feet. Open year-round.

Boone G.C., Boone
Mostly level fairways, with a creek coming into play on several holes.
Open April through November.

Cherokee Hills, Murphy
Immaculate, rolling course over former hunting ground of Cherokee
Indians. Packages available that include on-site accommodations. Also,
tennis, pool and restaurant on-site.

Crooked Creek G.C., Hendersonville
Built on the old Warner Brothers estate. A relatively flat course with
water on 13 of the 18 holes.

Cummings Cove G. & C.C., Hendersonville
Hidden gem designed by Robert Cupp. Well conditioned with beautiful
views. Part of a master-planned mountain residential community.

Fairfield Mountains Resort, Lake Lure
Apple Valley is a hilly, tight Dan Maples design with magnificent
mountain scenery. Bald Mountain is a challenging test with an abundance
of woods and water. Both courses are crisscrossed by trout streams. Part
of expansive timeshare resort. Must be a member or on-site guest to play.

Flat Rock G.C., Kenmure
Bentgrass from tee to green.

Grassy Creek G.C., Spruce Pine
Villa and home rentals on site, as well as restaurant and lounge.

Hanging Rock G. & C.C. at Seven Devils, Boone
Hilly, mountaintop course with dense woods.

High Meadows G. & C.C., Roaring Gap
Mountain layout with rolling terrain and substantial water.

Holly Forest C.C., Sapphire
Challenging course situated 3,400 feet above sea level.

Laurel Ridge C.C., Waynesville
Challenging, Bob Cupp-designed mountain course. Bring plenty of ammunition. Call pro shop for outside play policy.

Linville Ridge C.C., Linville
Highest course east of the Mississippi; extraordinary views. Ranked among the 10 best courses in the state. Call pro shop for guest play policy.

Lost Diamond Valley C.C., Flat Rock
Short, flat nine-hole layout that can be deceptively difficult. Meandering creeks add to the challenge.

Mill Creek Club, Franklin
Serene, rolling layout with gently contoured greens and rippling creeks. Golf packages available with on-site lodging and meeting rooms. Open year-round.

Mountain Harbour G.C., Hayesville
Scenic mountain course surrounded by national forest and 7,000-acre Lake Chatuge. Part of a private, equity country club community. Variety of homesites and condominiums available.

Red Fox C.C., Tryon
Packages available. Open year-round.

Springdale C.C., Canton
Front nine is hilly; back nine is flat. A creek meanders through the course, coming into play often. Golf packages available including accommodations and meals. Variety of real estate also available.

The seventh hole at Pinehurst No. 2 exudes a moody magnificence in the morning light.

PINEHURST

Pinehurst

The Complete List of Courses Open to the Public

Location	Course	Address
Aberdeen	**Legacy G.L.	P.O. Box 1158
	**The Pit G.L.	Highway 5
Jackson Springs	Foxfire C.C.—	
Pinebluff	*East Course	Hoffman Rd.
Pinehurst	West Course	Hoffman Rd.
	The Pines G.R.	Highway 1 S.
	Longleaf C.C.	2001 Midland Rd.
	Midland C.C. (9)	Midland Rd.
	Pinehurst R. & C.C.—	
	*No. 1 Course	Highway 15/501 N.
	**No. 2 Course	Highway 15/501 N.
	*No. 3 Course	Highway 15/501 N.
	*No. 4 Course	Highway 15/501 N.
	*No. 5 Course	Highway 15/501 N.
	**No. 6 Course	Highway 15/501 N.
	**No. 7 Course	Highway 15/501 N.
Robbins	Riverside C.C.	Box 428
Southern Pines	Hyland Hills C.C.	4100 Highway 1 N.
	Knollwood Fairways (9)	1470 Midland Rd.
	**Mid Pines C.C.	1010 Midland Rd.
	**Pine Needles G.C.	Midland Rd.
	*Southern Pines C.C. (27)	Country Club Dr.
	*Talamore at Pinehurst	1595 Midland Rd.
Vass	Woodlake C.C. (27)	Star Rd.
West End	Beacon Ridge	600 Longleaf Dr.
	Seven Lakes C.C.	Devonshire Rd.
Whispering Pines	C.C. of Whispering Pines—	
	*East Course	2 Clubhouse Blvd.
	West Course	2 Clubhouse Blvd.
	Whispering Woods C.C.	21 Cardinal Circle

* Recommended Course ** Highly Recommended

"When a pilgrim arrives in St. Andrews, Scotland, he is immediately accepted because he is a golfer. He will find a wonderful walking town, four quite wonderful golf courses, with dozens more nearby. He will breathe history back to the 14th century. He will see school children on bikes carrying golf clubs for an after-school round. Sacks of golf clubs will be lined against a wall in a pub as the locals munch on those doughy "filled rolls" and discuss anything pertaining to golf, the separation from England that must come, and the peculiar clothes American visitors wear. Fade out from the Kingdom of Fife, fade into a kingdom of golf in the pine forests of North Carolina in a geologically peculiar area known as the

Rating/Slope: Men	Women	Par	Cost	Phone
70.8/124	68.3/120	72	Moderate	(910) 944-8825
70.2/128	68.4/121	71	High	(910) 944-7069
70.7/129	70.5/119	72	Moderate	(910) 295-4563
71.0/123	70.4/115	72	Moderate	(910) 295-4563
na/121	—	72	Low	(910) 281-3165
67.3/110	65.7/108	72	Moderate	(910) 692-6100
66.9/110	68.5/110	35	Low	(910) 295-3241
67.4/114	70.1/117	72	High	(910) 295-8141
71.4/127	74.2/135	72	High	(910) 295-8141
67.2/112	70.1/114	71	High	(910) 295-8141
70.8/117	71.8/119	72	High	(910) 295-8141
71.2/123	74.7/131	72	High	(910) 295-8141
73.2/132	71.2/125	72	High	(910) 295-8141
73.7/142	69.7/124	72	Very High	(910) 295-8141
69.5/114	70.0/122	69	Low	(910) 464-3686
68.4/113	66.8/109	72	Moderate	(910) 692-3752
Executive	Executive	35	Low	(910) 692-3572
69.5/122	72.3/128	72	High	(910) 692-2114
70.2/126	68.4/118	71	High	(910) 692-7111
68.2/115	70.9/118	71	High	(910) 692-6551
70.8/134	69.0/125	71	High	(910) 692-4366
72.5/132	72.2/130	72	Moderate	(910) 245-4686
79.5/123	67.1/115	72	Moderate	(910) 673-2950
70.5/124	70.6/123	72	Moderate	(910) 672-1092
71.7/126	71.1/120	72	Moderate	(910) 949-2311
69.7/124	69.3/111	71	Moderate	(910) 949-2311
67.4/110	67.4/113	70	Low	(910) 949-4653

Sandhills. A pilgrim to Pinehurst, N.C. is immediately accepted because he is a golfer. He will discover a wonderful walking village lifted right out of England, and seven quite wonderful golf courses with several dozen more nearby. He will discover not kids on bikes, but an adult population whizzing around in golf cars, to the club, to the post office, and these same residents munching on corned beef on rye at the Village Deli, or humongous hamburgers at the Donald Ross Grill at the Country Club. They will be discussing anything relating to golf, the strange politics of this state, and the peculiar clothes European tourists wear."

That was the opening written by the great Dick Taylor for a piece on Pinehurst Resort & Country Club in the Summer 1992 issue of *Southern Links*. Rather than serving up a gushy, glad-handed tribute to this country's last great bastion of golf tradition, Taylor simply wrote from the heart about an area in which he has made his home for the past several years. His parallels to St. Andrews are eerily accurate, not the least bit contrived or exaggerated. If America can stake any claim to golf in the kingdom, it is among the sandhills of Pinehurst.

I was first introduced to Pinehurst as a young teenager, spending two summers at a two-week golf retreat run by Peggy Kirk Bell and her late husband Warren "Bullet" Bell at Pine Needles Resort. Since then, my visits have been all too infrequent; yet, there's an allure to the place that never leaves you. Maybe it's the surroundings, the deafening quiet save for the wind whispering through the Carolina pines. Maybe it's the fact that everything here— *everything*—revolves around golf. Maybe it's the genuine warmth of the people who, as Dick noted, make visitors feel welcome not because of an obligation to the local economy, but because of a mutual admiration and love for the game. Granted, Pinehurst is not for everyone. If you can't immerse yourself in several days of eating, drinking, laughing, talking, analyzing and experiencing nothing but golf, then perhaps you're better off somewhere where the diversions are a little more defined. Somewhere like, say, Hilton Head.

What exactly is it that has made the Pinehurst area synonymous with great golf? Is it the nearly 700 golf holes (or roughly 124 miles of fairways) stretched out among the 760 square miles of Moore County? Is it the magnificent PGA/World Golf Hall of Fame, which has been sadly shunned by the professional golf powers-that-be in favor of a more

Although water is almost completely absent from Pinehurst No. 2, Donald Ross's course at Pine Needles features some daunting carries. Pictured here is Pine Needles' par-4 fourth hole.

commercialized facility in Florida? Or is it because golfers from all corners of the world and of every stature have held Pinehurst in such high regard for nearly 100 years?

For most of us, it's all of this and more. But Pinehurst's standing in the world of golf can be suitably summarized in one word: tradition. Nestled among the quaint villages and towns in the Pinehurst area are the traditions that epitomize golf's grandest era. It was an era when legends were born and grew, with names like Jones, Sarazen, Nelson, Hagen,

One of the newest delights in the Sandhills is the Jack Nicklaus II-designed Legacy Golf Links, which offers this beautifully sculpted par-3 fifth hole as one of several along the water.

Zaharias, Hogan, Snead and Palmer. It was a time of craftsmanship and pride in handmade and hand-tooled golf clubs colorfully known as niblicks, brassies, mashies and spoons. And while the competition was fierce, it was competition in the true spirit of sport. This was a time of warmth, camaraderie and goodwill. And in that regard, time has stood still in Pinehurst.

A few years ago, I had the privilege of playing Pinehurst No. 2—the dowager of all courses here, due to celebrate its 100th birthday in a few years—in the company of Fletcher Gaines. Fletcher is the dean of the Pinehurst caddies and has the enviable distinction of having looped for the legendary designer Donald Ross, the transplanted Scot who turned Pinehurst into his own personal canvas in the early 1900s and lived here until his death in 1948. In the crisp early March morning, with the dew still draped across No. 2's hallowed corridors, Fletcher Gaines spoke very respectfully about "Mr. Ross" and his disdain for anyone, pro or amateur, breaking 70 on his course. "I'll fix 'em," he would say, and Fletcher, still hearing the words from Ross' lips like it was yesterday, let slip a grin as the sun broke through the morning chill.

There's only one way to play No. 2. And there's only one place for golf in the kingdom, American style.

Getting There

The Pinehurst area is located between Charlotte and Raleigh in south-central North Carolina, with easy access from Interstates 95, 85, and 40, and direct access from U.S. 1, U.S. 15-501, N.C. 211, N.C. 2, and N.C. 5. USAir has three flights daily connecting Charlotte to the Pinehurst/Southern Pines airport. Other commercial air service is available into Raleigh/Durham, Fayetteville and Greensboro. Amtrak service is also available, providing daily connections to New York, Miami or Tampa.

Climate

The Sandhills region enjoys pleasant temperatures year-round, with mild winters and cool, less humid summers. Rain disappears into the ground about as fast as it falls, so that outdoor sports can be enjoyed immediately after the rain ceases.

Activities

Those who don't come to Pinehurst for golf will find a few other diversions to keep them occupied. Horseback riders can arrange for mounts at Pinehurst Stables, where expert instruction is available for novices and superb mounts for experienced riders. They also offer

Above left: Rees Jones, in addition to his Pinehurst No. 7 course (and revisions at No. 4), designed the exciting Talamore at Pinehurst, seen here at the well-guarded 10th hole. Below: The 15th hole at Pinehurst No. 5, "The Cathedral Hole," was substantially revised by Robert Trent Jones.

carriage rides, which is a great way to tour the village, as well as pony rides for children. Tennis buffs will find nearly 100 courts in the area, and the Pinehurst Gun Club is a magnificent facility for trap and skeet shooting and sporting clays. Annie Oakley taught sharpshooting at the club around the turn of the century. There's also water sports and soaking up the sun (in season, preferably) at Lake Pinehurst, or simply browzing and window shopping in the village. Make sure to stop by the soda fountain at the drug store. About 10 miles north of Southern Pines is the little town of Cameron, which offers more than 60 antique shops.

Attractions

Cosider a trip to Seagrove, a little town about an hour north of Pinehurst on U.S. 220. This area has been turning out pottery for more than 200 years, and there are numerous potters who still hone their craft for the public. A mile north of town is the Potter's Museum, which chronicles the area's love affair with the art. Further north, in Asheboro, is the North Carolina Zoological Park, a 1,448-acre zoo with a variety of natural habitats for its species. So far, there's a magnificent Africa region with lions, elephants, chimpanzees, antelope and gazelles, and the R.J. Reynolds Forest Aviary with 150 exotic birds, trees and plants. There's a tram ride, a picnic area, a restaurant and gift shops. The zoo is open from April through October 15, and there is an admission charge.

Shopping

In both Pinehurst and Southern Pines, the shops are small, charming and filled with interesting, often exquisite items. Downtown Southern Pines, U.S. 1 in the Broad Street area, is a wonderful collection of shops and restaurants in the historic district. Less than five miles south on U.S. 1 in Aberdeen is the Aberdeen Exchange, a crafts/farmers market in the town's historic district.

Popular Dining Options

All the resorts have excellent dining, but a visit to Pinehurst wouldn't be complete without a stop at the *Pine Crest Inn*, a small but legendary hangout of some of golfdom's best-known writers and players. If you think you've spotted golf scribes like Dick Taylor, Bob Drum, or Charles Price at one of the tables in the back...well, you probably have. The adjoining lounge is small but justly famed as a *19th Hole*. *The Greenhouse Restaurant* is a light, airy eatery with house specialties, great soups and desserts, but open for lunch only. In Southern Pines, try *Antoine's* for French cuisine in an intimate setting, or a local favorite, the *Lob Steer Inn*. Finally, *Morrie's Deli and Bakery* is a great lunch spot—and the portions are more than ample.

For More Information

The Pinehurst Area Convention & Visitors Bureau, P.O. Box 2270, Southern Pines, NC 28388, (910) 692-3330 or (800) 346-5362.

THE RESORTS IN DEPTH

Mid Pines Resort
"Vintage Ross in a Subtle Sandhills Classic"

You don't have to write a 10,000-word dissertation on the architectural theories of Donald Ross in order to fully appreciate Mid Pines Resort.

What you do need to know is how to draw your golf ball into a fairway that pitches hard to the right so it will hold, or how to cut a fairway wood on a par-five to avoid pitching over a bunker. Basically you need to know how to think your way around a golf course. But that's the beauty of Ross. He doesn't overpower you with length, he just makes it important to hit the shot he's asking you to hit.

Mid Pines Resort of Pinehurst measures just over 6,500 yards from the blue tees and at last check hasn't sent anybody to an ATM machine for more golf-ball money or to the 19th Hole for comfort. Yet the patrons keep returning year after year. Each April, nearly all of the club's 200 daily tee times are booked.

The golf course won't dazzle you, nor will the resort itself or its host of amenities. What both will do, however, is serve up enough comfort,

Mid Pines, built in 1910 by Donald Ross, has never been remodeled and thus offers a rare opportunity to play a Ross course in its original design.

smiles and charm that bells and whistles aren't needed to keep the customers happy. Typical of the attitude at the 72-year-old resort is the approach one former general manager used in squelching complaints from some elderly ladies about having to climb two flights of stairs. The resort didn't have an elevator, and when one woman asked the manager why she was assigned to the third floor, he told her that they were putting all the younger women on the third floor. She walked off completely satisfied.

Mid Pines uses that same attitude today to carve its niche in the Sandhills golf and travel economy. Located on Midland Road one mile from Southern Pines and four miles from the Pinehurst Resort & Country Club, the resort offers its vintage Donald Ross golf course, meeting and banquet facilities, three meals a day, and a variety of recreational activities. It has recently undergone a half-million-dollar renovation that upgraded the dining room, lobby and common areas.

Mid Pines is a direct spin-off of the popularity that the Pinehurst Hotel & Club enjoyed during its first quarter-century. Ross had designed four courses at Pinehurst by 1919 and Richard Tufts, grandson of Pinehurst founder James W. Tufts, noted in his unpublished history of the area that up to 15,000 people were being turned down for reservations during the months of February and March. That led to the inception in 1921 of Mid Pines.

Later purchased and expanded by the Cosgrove family (Frank Cosgrove and his wife Maisie had been long-time Pinehurst employees), Mid Pines gained tremendous exposure when one of the Cosgrove daughters married an accountant from Southern Pines named Julius Boros, who promptly became the head pro, set a course record of 62 which stands today, and went on to star on the PGA Tour, bringing home two U.S. Opens among his many trophies. During the period, many of golf's greats came through Mid Pines—their pictures hang on the walls of the Mid Pines recreation room and pro shop today—from Snead to Hogan to Palmer to Zaharias.

One guest through the years was Stewart Bainum, the president and chairman of Quality Inns. He became so enamored with the resort that in 1973, when the Cosgroves were aging and none of the daughters cared to take it over, he bought Mid Pines. It has remained in Quality Inn's hands ever since and is a member of Quality's Clarion chain of upscale resorts.

Despite that big-business affiliation, Mid Pines works hard to maintain the easy-going atmosphere the Cosgroves instilled more than four decades ago. A hostess bids a diner goodnight with, "Glad you enjoyed it, dear." A locker room attendant cleans your golf shoes and replaces your spikes. The golf shop can line up a caddy with a day's notice. The convention services staff can arrange any frill for a group, from bringing in a hot-air balloon to booking Chubby Checker.

But what's most important at Mid Pines—indeed, in all the Pinehurst area—is golf. And though livelier balls and fortified clubs make the game a bit different than when Ross and construction chief Frank Maples built it, Mid Pines has held up well over time and is an afternoon well spent. The championship route is 6,515 yards, the regular one 6,121 yards, and the ladies travel 5,592 yards. Unlike many Ross courses, Mid Pines remains basically the way the designer laid it out . Some tees have been elongated, and some bunkers covered over, but it remains basically the way Ross put it there.

Mid Pines is a thinking man's adventure, beginning with the 414-yard third hole, a dogleg right. The bend in the hole is relatively close to the tee, and between the 150-yard marker and the green is a pond that encroaches from the right. Play the white tees and hit driver, and you can easily hit it through the fairway, or hit the requisite fade and it could find the water. The smart play is four-wood off the tee and accept the little longer approach. Then there are several short par-fours that require patience (i.e. thought; i.e., less than driver) off the tee. The premium on driving is so important, because the fairways tend to slope toward trouble, or the landing areas are very small. The only real scoring opportunities at Mid Pines are on its par-fives. Typical of Ross courses, the fives are all fairly short and relatively reachable in two. Nos. 5 and 15, for instance, play less than 500 yards from the tips.

Ross saved the best hole for last. No. 18 is a par-four of 411 yards that slopes down from the tee, then gradually inclines the last quarter of the way up to the green. It requires a straight or slightly drawn shot from an elevated tee, then a mid-iron off a slight downslope. The green sits in a bowl that leads up to the hotel. It is certainly one of the area's prettiest holes, and a gorgeous way to finish the round. And it leaves you asking for more....typical of Ross. And typical of Mid Pines.

Pine Needles
"A Legacy of Southern Hospitality"

Peggy Kirk Bell walks onto the Pine Needles practice tee on a Monday morning and stares down the dozen or so men whom she'll be teaching golf for five days. Half kiddingly, half prophetically, she sneers at them and says," Man, am I going to enjoy telling you what to do."

For Bell, a charter member of the LPGA, former pilot, mother of three

Top: Pine Needles' cozy environment makes it a favorite with repeat visitors to Pinehurst. Below right: The par-3 third hole at Pine Needles plays short, but features a sharply sloped green that puts placement at a premium.

and Pine Needles owner and director of golf, the good-natured implication is that she is indeed in charge here. Even if she is smack in the middle of a rustic, hunting lodge-of-a-golf-resort built specifically for foursomes and eightsomes of men. This is her home, her area of expertise, and her love. And she's not about to take any macho guff from a man. Especially when she can probably outdrive and outscore every single one of them.

She will have fun with them, though. Just as she has been doing with thousands of golf-hungry students since 1953, the year she and her husband bought the Pine Needles golf course in Southern Pines, 10 minutes down the road from Pinehurst.

Built in the 1920s by the Tufts family (owners of the Pinehurst resort), Pine Needles had fallen on hard times during the Depression era and during the Second World War, when the hotel was commandeered by the army.

Enter the Bells. Peggy, a Curtis Cup team member in 1948 and 1950, gave up her tour career in 1953 to marry her hometown sweetheart, Warren "Bullet" Bell. That same year they joined the Cosgrove family and Julius Boros, both family friends, in purchasing the Pine Needles golf course. They didn't buy the old hotel, though. It is owned by the Catholic Church and is used as a hospital.

Today, Pine Needles guests are housed in free-standing, five-bedroom lodges (four bedrooms and a hospitality room) built by "Bullet" Bell. The foursomes or

Visions and revisions at Pinehurst. Top left: Dan Maples recently converted an old equestrian center into the the hilly and often windy Longleaf course. Below left: Pinehurst No. 2 has been revised no less than ten times, including seven stages of addition and revision by Donald Ross, to achieve the subtle contours in evidence here at the 15th hole.

eightsomes that occupied the lodges could stay up as late as they cared, yet be separated from other, less party-minded guests. The individual bedrooms could also be locked-out, and sold to singles or couples as hotel rooms.

Until his death in 1984 it was Bullet that drove the car at Pine Needles. A man of conviction with a bite worse than his bark, Bullet roamed the 450-acre property with an eagle eye and uncommon energy. Since 1984 it has been the incandescent and unflappable Peg Bell behind the steering wheel. Although she took the loss of her husband hard, her love of the game ultimately brought her back.

The Pine Needles 18 is a par-71 whose fairways flow across the rolling Sandhills of south-central North Carolina. Built with elbow grease and oxen in 1927, the course doesn't have a contrived square foot on it. It even has the same aesthetic feel of decades ago. Weathered and rudimentary wood signs serve as tee markers. And of the handful of fairway homes that sprinkle the course, many look as if they predate the course. During the season the course is reserved exclusively for guests of the 67-room property. No outside play is allowed. You don't make the turn at 9; you make it at 18 (perfectly suited to playing 36 holes a day), expedited by a lavish yet efficient lunch buffet served in the clubhouse. The shoulders of the course are well groomed to keep your ball in sight and speed up play. And Pine Needles has never offered local memberships, so there are no member times to book around.

The front nine of Rees Jones' No. 7 course at Pinehurst finishes on this devilish little par-three.

Peggy Kirk Bell will tell you that Pine Needles is a shotmaker's course. She also admits that, until recently, technology had taken some of that shotmaking out of play on several holes. Design features that Ross had built into the course in the '20s were being carried by the longer tee shots of the '90s. A good example is the 396-yard, par-4 fourth hole. In Ross' day the landing area was 180-200 yards out and called for a tee shot that would hug the left center line of the fairway or be cast into the woods on the right because of a sharp side slope. Until recently you could fly that section of the fairway and take it out of play. But Pine Needles has pushed back the tee on No. 4, and on several other holes, in order to bring those design features back into consideration.

Although Pine Needles doesn't carry the same top-of-mind awareness of other fellow *Golf Digest* Top 75 resort courses, it has had its share of glory. It hosted the 1991 USGA Senior Women's Open, and will host the 1996 Women's U.S. Open.

The future of golf instruction at Pine Needles is equally bright. Bell has gathered a strong supporting cast to join her. She has brought on Dr. Jim Suttie, the man credited with guiding Paul Azinger's swing to Tour caliber. Suttie has developed a computer program that demonstrates the strengths and weaknesses of a student's golf swing through video analysis. Bell also has Senior PGA Tour pro Harvie Ward helping with course strategy and senior clinics, plus son-in-law and Pine Needles touring pro Pat McGowan working the line during his off weeks.

Bell, however, is the anchor of the resort's instructional program. Considered one of the five most influential women in the sport, she has been the recipient of countless industry accolades including the 1989 Ellen Griffin Award bestowed by the teaching division of the LPGA, and the USGA's Bobby Jones Award, which recognizes her overall contributions to the sport.

Golf instruction is important at Pine Needles because golf is important to Peggy Kirk Bell. The quality of the instruction and the quality of the course are representative of the way things are handled at Pine Needles. Peg wants them just right, and she doesn't mind telling you what to do to get them that way.

Pinehurst Resort & C.C.
"The Tradition Lives On At America's Grand Golf Resort"

Had it not been for the enterprising inventor of the soda fountain, a creative Yankee, and a disgruntled dairyman, golf in Pinehurst might never have gotten off the ground. Or off the tee, as it were.

Changing times in Pinehurst. Above: Built in 1979 by George and Tom Fazio, the No. 6 course brought a completely new look to the Pinehurst Resort line-up. Pictured here, the 17th hole. **Top:** There isn't much that Dan Maples *didn't* try at The Pit, including quarry holes, blind shots, and this island green on the back nine.

As the oft-told story has it, James Walker Tufts, the Boston soda-fountain magnate, purchased 5,000 acres of ravaged timberland in the North Carolina Sandhills in 1895. Many thought Tufts to be a fool, shelling out good money ($1 an acre) for such barren, sandy wasteland. Yet Tufts, perhaps the first semblance of a modern-day developer, envisioned something special for his investment. He set out to build a quaint little New England-style village that would serve as a winter resort for his fellow frostbitten Yankees.

For the first few months, Tufts' Southern Retreat was known as "Tuftown." Realizing that the name lacked the appeal he was looking for, Tufts initiated a contest at his summer home on Martha's Vineyard to rename his North Carolina development. One local entrant submitted a catchy name that combined the native woodlands with "hurst," a reference to to a sandy piece of rising ground. Nice ring to it. "Pinehurst" was born.

Many scribes have labeled Pinehurst as "the golf capital of the world." However trite the phrase, it probably still holds true. In terms of sheer facilities, Pinehurst Country Club is the largest single golf complex in the world. It contains seven golf courses; three clubhouses; a golf shop that resembles a small department store; indoor and outdoor instructional facilities with a renowned year-round golf school; and a beautiful racquet club designed, as the great golf writer Charles Price once said, "for people who might go to Wimbledon for golf."

The Pinehurst hotel, originally built as The Carolina in 1901, is an awe-inspiring site, nestled at the end of a long tree-lined lane in the heart of Pinehurst. Despite extensive renovations over the years, the 318-room hotel retains all of the Southern charm and grace of its early days. The service is impeccable; the furnishings elegant; the dining extraordinary. Surrounded by immaculately maintained grounds, splashed with colorful azaleas, camellias and dogwoods, the Pinehurst Hotel perhaps best represents the perfect balance between progress and tradition.

The par-4 second hole on Pinehurst's No. 2 course looks tame, but in fact it's one of the toughest, most subtle par-4s in the area. Only a superbly-played approach shot will leave any meaningful chance for birdie.

The Pinehurst tradition is built around the resort's remarkable facilities. Dubbed "The Magnificent Seven," the Pinehurst Country Club courses represent the works of some of golf's most respected designers - Donald Ross, Ellis Maples, Robert Trent Jones, George and Tom Fazio, and Rees Jones. Each course has its own character and personality and although all aren't as challenging as Ross' fabled No. 2 course, there is a layout suitable to every conceivable level of play.

After opening the initial nine holes at Pinehurst, Tufts hired Ross, a young Scottish professional, in 1901 to direct his golf operations. Over the next 20 years, Ross built courses 2, 3 and 4 at Pinehurst. The sandy soil reminded Ross of his native Scotland and, ever the perfectionist, he constantly made renovations to the courses to retain their unique character. While such frequent revisions are often viewed negatively, the changes made to the Pinehurst courses have only served to enhance their character and playability. No. 2, regarded as Ross' true masterpiece, has been revised no less than nine times. No. 4 has been changed by both Robert Trent and Rees Jones over the past 25 years, and No. 5, built by Maples as a long and demanding complement to No. 2 in 1961, was later refined by Robert Trent Jones.

With such an amalgamation of designers and styles, it's no mystery why Pinehurst offers an allure to golfers of all skill levels. There is truly something for everyone there.

Nos. 1 and 3 at Pinehurst are favorites of the club's members. Both are short (5,852 and 5,956 yards, respectively, from the championship tees) yet scenic layouts that wind through dense stands of loblolly and longleaf pines.

Despite its numerous facelifts, Pinehurst No. 4 remains the resort's sleeper course. Robert Trent Jones toughened the original course in 1973 for the PGA's World Open, and son Rees scaled the course back to more playable standards in the winter of 1983. The course plays from 5,726 to 6,878 yards and features some of the most scenic holes in the entire Sandhills area.

No. 5 also varies in length, from 5,832 to 6,827 yards, but features more water hazards - eight - than any of the other six courses. It also rivals No. 2 in the number of sand bunkers with 55. The 175-yard, par-three 15th on No. 5, dubbed the "Cathedral Hole," is one of the most photographed holes at Pinehurst. The hole plays from an elevated tee across a pond to a small green enveloped by towering pines.

Pinehurst Nos. 6 and 7 rival No. 2 as the favorites of the resort's guests. Carved from the rolling sandhills, No. 6 offers golfers all of the traditional Fazio touches—undulating fairways, an abundance of swales and mounding, devilish water hazards, and heavily bunkered greens. At the time of its construction, No. 6 also presented Pinehurst with a new degree of difficulty in length: 7,098 yards from the back tees with a hefty rating of 74.5 and a 139 slope.

The Fazios seemed to have the market cornered on drama at Pinehurst until Rees Jones unveiled his infamous No. 7 course in 1986. In terms of sheer length and flat-out challenge from tee to green, the monstrous No. 7 is without compare. Should anyone dare to venture toward the back tees, they'll find 7,114 yards, a 75.0 rating and a 145 slope.

Jones, one of the game's most imaginative designers, threw in a little bit of everything on No. 7: Scottish-style swales and pot bunkers, massive elevation changes that rival the most mountainous of layouts, and marshes and streams reminiscent of a coastal area. Seven is a driver's course, with a great deal of finesse required around the elevated greens. By keeping many of the course's natural areas intact, Jones has given the course somewhat of a Pine Valley feel, particularly on the back nine.

The cornerstone of Pinehurst Country Club is the storied No. 2 course. Perennially ranked as one of the greatest courses in the world, No. 2 is a monument to the design genius of Donald Ross. Ross once referred to No. 2 as the "fairest test of championship golf I have ever designed." Tom Fazio has said that "from 40 yards in to the green, No. 2 is perhaps the finest golf course in the world."

At 7,020 yards from the championship tees, No. 2 presents the ultimate challenge for all facets of one's game with deceptively wide fairways, roughs dotted with love grass, and small, firm greens. The greens at No. 2, like those on many other Ross courses, slope away to the sides and back to create a much smaller target area. Additionally, Ross' preservation of natural undulations in front of the greens often disguise the distance to the flag. Add the ever-present swirling winds at No. 2, and you have a golf course which requires intense concentration on every shot.

Golf is indeed played, spoken, eaten, and drunk at Pinehurst Country Club, from the hotel's formal dining room (where jackets are still required at dinner) to the 91st Hole pub in the main clubhouse. But one may also choose to ramble around the quaint Pinehurst village that was originally designed by Frederick Law Olmstead, the same gentleman who created New York's Central Park. The village is filled with specialty shops and boutiques. There's a library, where one can spend hours poring over the Tufts family archives. The locals swap stories and gossip at the Post Office or the drug store which, incidentally, features a real soda fountain—no doubt a lasting tribute to old man Tufts.

Although No. 2 has hosted many professional and amateur tournaments through the years—including the Ryder Cup, the PGA Championship, the U.S. Men's and Women's Amateur championships, and the prestigious North and South Amateur (92 years and counting)—the U.S. Open will finally be played at Pinehurst in 1999, after the positive experiences of the 1992-93 Tour Championship.

As much as Pinehurst deserves the U.S. Open, the Open deserves Pinehurst. For there is arguably nowhere else in the U.S. that commands such worldwide recognition and respect of golf's grand traditions. Pinehurst Country Club will always cast a spell over its visitors. Take an early morning stroll over No. 2 with the pine needles crunching underfoot and the wind whispering through the towering pines, and you'll understand. Old man Tufts would be proud of his Pinehurst. It just gets better with age.

The Pit
"Sixty Years In The Making, And Worth The Wait"

Many an adjective has been used to describe The Pit, the Dan Maples 18-hole creation tucked into the heart of the Pinehurst sandhills. They tend to range from the praiseworthy to the profane.

This is not to say that The Pit is unworthy of proper kudos. On the contrary, the course has drawn rave reviews since its opening in 1985, not bad considering the stature of some its high-falutin' neighbors. *Golf Digest* has included The Pit among its Top 50 Public Courses for several years, and *Golf* magazine has regarded its par-5 eighth hole as one of the top golf holes in America. There have even been comparisons to Pine Valley. The Pit carries a subhead as "A Dan Maples Original." That sounds a little contrived, but it is actually a magnificent understatement. Maples, if you don't already know by now, is the son of famed golf course architect Ellis Maples and the grandson of legendary course builder Frank Maples, who built courses for Donald Ross just down the road at Pinehurst Resort & Country Club. Dan Maples has already been lauded for his designs in the Myrtle Beach, S.C. area—most notable are Oyster Bay, Marsh Harbour, Sea Trail and the Pearl Golf Links. Having conquered the golf-crazy Grand Strand in the early 1980s, Maples moved back to his family's old stomping grounds and created one of the most talked-about, and offtimes cursed, golf courses in the entire Sandhills area.

Maples sculpted The Pit out of a 230-acre commercial sand quarry used for mining purposes since the 1920s. The commercial operations were abandoned in 1975, and the land remained virtually unused until Maples arrived in 1984. Through extraordinary vision, he found the jutting dunes, dense pine forests and extreme natural undulation to be a prime venue for his work. In just 13 months, Maples shaped this vast, rugged terrain into a totally unconventional, yet highly refreshing, golf experience. Perhaps more than anything else, The Pit represents Maples' ability, and willingness, to overcome all imaginable limitations imposed by nature to create a stunning piece of work. It's highly unlikely that the topography of the golf course could be recreated, even in this day and age of moving umpteen million cubic yards of earth. There are countless rows of towering mounds and natural dunes on the site, many of which have been there for 60 years. The course is breathtakingly beautiful, in a very rugged sort of way.

The Pit features four sets of tees, ranging from 4,759 yards to 6,600 yards from the championship box. Though the course isn't long by normal standards, the tight serpentine fairways and small, undulating bentgrass greens demand accuracy all the way around. The slope rating from the tips is an enormous 139, making it almost inconceivable that the course record is nine-under par 63.

The layout of The Pit is bedeviling in itself. The first two holes follow the more traditional Donald Ross design of other Pinehurst area courses, but the 355-yard par-4 third plays sharply uphill to an undulating green surrounded by original waste areas that were once used extensively for mining. No. 4 is a scenic 172-yard par-three, flanked from tee to green by steep mounds. Nos. 4, 5 and 6 revert back to standard Sandhills-type character, but the real fun begins at the 480-yard, par-5 eighth. No. 8 represents the first true "pit" feel of the golf course. From the elevated tee, one gets the impression that No. 8 is easily reachable in two shots. But the narrow, winding fairway is flanked on both sides by what one wag once described as a "battlefield:" rows of scarred, brushy mounds that give way to dense pine forests. Naturally, keeping the ball in play is paramount in order to get close in two. The approach, though short, requires extreme finesse. The rolling green features a solitary pine situated directly at front left, and a steep drop into thick underbrush to the rear. Miss the green and you'll likely find the need for various implements not normally found in the standard golf bag.

The 430-yard par-4 ninth plays uphill, almost always into the wind, to an amphitheatre-like setting around the green. There are no sand bunkers on Nos. 8 or 9 - there are only 28 on the entire course - but there's no real need for them.

The 390-yard par-four 10th at The Pit is a relatively short dogleg right with a long, deep crevice of love grass bordering the entire right side and winding around in front of the green. Nos. 11 through 13 are built around the course's only water hazard, a 30-acre lake once used to wash the freshly mined sand. The eye-catcher here is the 167-yard par-three 12th, reminiscent of the 17th at the TPC at Sawgrass with an island green that's surrounded on three sides by a deep sand bunker.

The four finishing holes truly epitomize the unique character of The Pit, with the 540-yard par-five 15th serving as one of the premier holes in the entire Sandhills area. Like No. 8, the hole originates from a tee so elevated that you can almost view the rest of the golf course. The narrow fairway runs relatively straight until about 100 yards out, where it takes a wickedly sharp turn to the right. From there, the player is presented with perhaps the most demanding shot on the golf course: a pitch to a postage-stamp-sized green, severely undulating and partially hidden by crusty dunes and craggy pines. Should you get anywhere near the pocketed green in two - a feat in itself - the utmost precision is required to get down in regulation.

The 100-yard par-three 16th, played into a narrow valley, may seem like a breath of fresh air following the previous test, but anything stronger than a half-wedge will find a wall of underbrush beckoning to the rear. On 17, a 381-yard par-four, and 18, a 535-yard par-five, the tight landing areas require more accuracy than power off the tee. Finding a stray drive in the surrounding sandy brush isn't as difficult as it may seem. Playing out, however, is another story.

Despite the rough, scarred nature of The Pit, the foliage covering the mounds actually turns a lush green in the spring and summer months. In the fall, indigenous wildflowers bloom throughout the roughs to make The Pit even more breathtaking. But whatever the time of year, chances are The Pit will leave you muttering to yourself. The choice of words is entirely up to you.

ALSO IN THE AREA

Beacon Ridge C.C.
Short, not overly taxing Gene Hamm design (4,730-6,511 yards) built in 1988. A semi-private club, Beacon Ride is open for limited outside play.

C.C. of Whispering Pines
A relatively older pair of courses from Ellis Maples. The West Course is par-71 and though just over 6,300 yard from the back tees, is no pushover. But the real challenge is the par-72 East Course which, at a whopping 7,138 from the tips, has all the length that anyone could want. A semi-private club, Whispering Pines is open for limited outside play.

Foxfire C.C.
An earlier (1968) design by Gene Hamm, Foxfire has two courses, East and West. East is slightly longer and slightly more difficult than the West course, but both are filled with challenge and are particularly daunting from the back tees, where West rates 72.8, and the East course an impressive 73.5.

Hyland Hills Resort
A resort course from Tom Jackson, this 1971 design is one of the easier courses in the Sandhills, and is particularly forgiving from the short (4,703 yards) forward tees.

Knollwood Fairways
Relatively flat but pleasant nine-holer on the road between Pinehurst and Southern Pines. Designed by Tom O'Neal in 1964, this is a friendly, executive-length course that's ideal for family groups and beginners.

Legacy G.L.
One of the newest and most popular daily-fee courses in the area, the Legacy is a twenty-minute drive out of town, but it well worth the extra effort. This is the second course designed by Jack Nicklaus II ,who won

the North and South Amateur in Pinehurst in 1985 before joining his father's architectural firm. It's a hilly, challenging winner that is relatively short from the forward tees and quite a challenge from the tips.

Longleaf C.C.

Definitely a change of pace for Dan Maples after designing The Pit, Longleaf is a pleasant, traditionally designed residential course built on a former equestrian facility (elements of which have been blended into the design). A relatively short and easy course, Longleaf has the Pinehurst bark without some of the Pinehurst bite.

Midland Farms C.C.

A 1977 design by Tom Jackson, on the road between Southern Pines and Pinehurst, this is a short and fun par-70 course well suited to the shorter-hitters. A semi-private course, Midland is open to limited outside play.

The Pines Resort

Overshadowed by its neighbors in Pinehurst, The Pines in nearby Pinebluff was designed by Frank Hicks and Russell Breeden and opened for play in 1971. At 4,588 from the forward tees, it offers some real scoring opportunities from the front, but packs some punch from the 6,617-yard back tees.

Riverside C.C.

Just up the road from Pinehurst, this is a friendly, eminently playable design by Porter Gibson, who formerly teamed up with Bob Toski. A semi-private club, Riverside is open to limited outside play.

Seven Lakes C.C.

Designed by Peter Tufts, godson of Donald Ross and the latest in the line of Pinehurst's founding family to take up golf design, this is a tough, fair, fairly lengthy course which will be tough on novices. A semi-private club, Seven Lakes is open to limited outside play.

Southern Pines C.C.

One of the earliest Donald Ross designs in Pinehurst (or anywhere for that matter), dating back to 1910, this course probably has the best claim as a Pinehurst hidden gem. It's conditioning hasn't always been the best, but the layout is first-rate. Well worth a detour, especially for Ross aficionados. A semi-private club, Southern Pines Country Club is open to limited outside play.

Talamore at Pinehurst

This is one of the courses that Pinehurst insiders have been touting since it opened in 1991. It's mighty tough—though easier than Jones' Pinehurst No. 7—but it is eminently fair. Top drawer Pinehurst golf from a top-drawer designer.

Whispering Woods G.C.

An interesting, playable course designed by Ellis Maples and opened in 1974, it's also one of the first courses co-credited to Dan Maples. Formerly known as the South Course at the C.C. of Whispering Pines, this semi-private course is open to limited outside play.

Woodlake C.C.

Originally known as the Lake Surf C.C., this club features 18 holes by Ellis Maples opened in 1969, and whopping par-40, 3,820 yard third nine by Dan Maples. It's one of the most unusual father/son collaborations around. A semi-private club, Woodlake is open for limited outside play.

NORTH CARC

The 18th hole at Nags Head Golf Links.

LINA COAST

North Carolina (

The Complete List of Courses Open to the Public

Location	Course	Address
Bald Head Island	**Bald Head Island C.C.	8 Bald Head Wind
Hampstead	*Belvedere Plantation G. & C.C.	2368 Country Club Dr.
	Olde Point G.C.	P.O. Box 249
	*Topsail Greens	Highway 17 N.
Kitty Hawk	Duck Woods C.C.	50 Dogwood Trail
	**Sea Scape G.C.	300 Eckner
Morehead City	Brandywine Bay	Highway 70 W. Route 2
Nags Head	**Nags Head G.L.	P.O. Box 1719
New Bern	*The Emerald G.C.	5000 Clubhouse Dr.
Sneads Ferry	North Shore G.C.	P.O. Box 841
Swansboro	Silver Creek G.C.	Highway 58
Wilmington	*Beau Rivage Plantation	6230 Carolina Beach Rd.
	*The Cape G. & R.C.	535 The Cape Blvd.
	Echo Farms G. & C.C.	4114 Echo Farms Blvd.

* Recommended Course ** Highly Recommended

THE CAPE FEAR COAST
(Wilmington to New Bern)

IT MAY NOT HAVE THE RAW ROMANTICISM OF ITS NEIGHBORS TO the north on the Outer Banks, but the southern coast of North Carolina – stretching from its furthest point south near Wilmington up to Beaufort and inland to New Bern – is unmatched in the state for sheer coastal beauty, intriguing history and seemingly boundless activity.

The entire Cape Fear region is dotted with stringy, narrow islands of vast, unspoiled beaches guarded by rustic lighthouses. Just a ferry ride away are the many quaint bay towns scattered along the coast with their colorful fishing boats and magnificently restored homes. Here you'll find some of the richest history south of Plymouth Rock and some of the best fishing on the entire eastern Seaboard.

This is a North Carolina that is often overshadowed by the Smoky Mountain region or the Outer Banks some 200 miles to the north. Golfers are almost assuredly unaware of the hidden treasures that lie among the rocky shoals and the maritime forests of the Cape Fear coast. And while the area isn't abundant in golf courses, quality easily surpasses quantity.

ɔast

Rating/Slope: Men	Women	Par	Cost	Phone
71.3/136	69.5/121	72	High	(910) 457-7310
69.5/125	69.1/117	71	Moderate	(910) 270-2703
69.6/122	69.1/115	72	Low	(910) 270-2403
69.0/118	69.1/114	71	Moderate	(910) 270-2883
69.4/129	70.7/123	72	High	(919) 261-2609
67.9/109	60.5/114	72	High	(919) 261-2158
70.0/115	70.4/113	71	Moderate	(919) 247-2541
66.9/126	64.7/117	71	High	(919) 441-8073
71.8/124	71.3/119	72	Moderate	(919) 633-4440
71.6/133	69.6/122	72	Moderate	(910) 327-2410
71.1/117	68.1/110	72	Moderate	(919) 393-8058
69.9/129	67.1/114	72	Moderate	(910) 392-9022
70.1/126	65.4/115	72	Moderate	(910) 799-3110
70.4/125	70.1/121	72	Moderate	(910) 791-9318

Technically, Wilmington isn't even on the coast—it's inland a bit, at the junction of the Cape Fear River's northeast and northwest branches. Nevertheless—despite the severe shoals that once guarded the mouth of the river—Wilmington developed into an important port during Colonial days and continued to play a major role during both world wars. The town has since grown steadily as a commercial shipping center, and in recent years has seen the development of a thriving new industry—some 34 movies have been filmed in the area, including *Crimes of the Heart* and *Blue Velvet*.

Remnants of the city's history are meticulously maintained in the old residential section of town. Nearby on the coast is Wrightsville Beach, a well-known family-oriented resort area, and Bald Head Island, a pristine barrier island that is wonderfully devoid of modern-day distractions. Both are perfect for swimming, fishing, beach combing, boating and creative loafing. The golf at Bald Head—discussed in greater detail later in this section—is the finest in this particular region.

Some 90 miles up the coast are the port towns of Beaufort and Morehead City. Beaufort (pronounced *Bo*-fort) is North Carolina's third-oldest town and still reflects its early history. Along its narrow streets are homes that date back to the late 1700s, and self-guided tours through the town's Historic Site features several 18th and 19th century landmarks. But

The 9th green at Nags Head Golf Links.

perhaps the city's most popular attraction is the state-owned North Carolina Maritime Museum, which in August hosts one of the country's most offbeat events, the Strange Seafood Festival. It's a golden opportunity to munch on marinated octopus, squid, stingray casserole

and other delicacies, and it's become so popular that you must reserve in advance.

Morehead City is renowned for fishing—the Gulfstream brings in an abundance of blue marlin, tarpon and other prizes. The inshore fishing is equally rewarding. There are some 80 miles of surf and 400 miles of protected waterways in the region.

Less than 50 miles inland is New Bern, which for several years served as the colonial capital. It is also the site of one of the most elegant mansions in the country—the Tryon Palace. An elegant 48-room complex built in 1767-70 by the former royal governor, the Palace was beautifully restored in the 1950s.

All the towns along the Cape Fear Coast are fairly accessible, provided you don't mind two-lane roads winding through old fishing villages under huge, old water oaks, emerging at intervals for long, straight patches of marshy sea-grass savannahs. It sounds appealing, and if it doesn't sound to you like North Carolina, then perhaps you don't know what you're missing.

THE OUTER BANKS

VACATIONERS FROM THE NORTHEAST, HAVING LONG BEEN USED TO such holiday hubs as Virginia Beach and Myrtle Beach, have in recent years discovered the Outer Banks, a narrow, splintered chain of islands that shields the North Carolina mainland from the whims of nature, where crowds are still at a minimum and commercialism is still a relatively naughty word.

Sure, you'll find rustic little souvenir shops, raw bars, t-shirt and shell vendors scattered along the highway that bisects Nags Head, the largest resort in the Outer Banks area. But it's all very beachy, quintessentially laid back. In fact, from the casual looks of things, you would never guess that Nags Head was once a fashionable summer retreat among North Carolina's wealthy plantation owners. The salt air, ocean breezes and sea water were thought to prevent the warm weather scourge of malaria.

The years between the Civil War and World War II marked the area's heyday. In 1838, a sumptuous hotel, replete with grand ballroom, was built to accommodate the annual influx of aristocrats seeking good health and good times. These early habitués of Nags Head erected large oceanfront cottages perched on pilings, with unpainted wood sidings and massive bench-lined porches. Thus emerged the Nags Head style: plain, functional and oblivious to wind and sea.

Although the cottages still stand, reminding natives of a genteel bygone era, the hotel is but a faint memory. In 1862, Confederate troops encamped at Nags Head, with the hotel serving as headquarters. When Union troops captured the island, the grand dame of Outer Banks high society was set ablaze by the Confederates to preclude it from being used by the enemy.

But Nags Head proved to be a resilient resort. Although the Civil War had cleaned out the fortunes of many North Carolina planters, a good number of them were able to resume their halcyon summer holidays on the Outer Banks, as if nothing had happened. Soon a new, albeit less lavish, hotel was built and new cottages cropped up. Slowly, as World War II approached, the Old Guard and their mannered lifestyle began to disappear. Nags Head was fast becoming a populist watering hole.

For buffs, this region has a formidable supply of history. Just up the road from Nags Head is the legendary town of Kitty Hawk. It was in 1903 that the Wright brothers came to this bleak spot to make the world's first successful power-driven airplane flight. They were attracted to Kitty Hawk because it offered a favorable wind velocity and a barren, sandy landscape, perfect for obstacle-free take-offs and soft landings.

On neighboring Roanoke Island, you can get lost in the mystique of the "Lost Colony." As any Southerner who made through the fourth grade will recall, it was on this lush island that 115 English colonists settled in 1587, only to disappear without a trace. At Fort Raleigh, you can stroll through the very site of the ill-fated colonists' settlement, engulfed by an eerie silence, save for a breeze that whispers through the pines and maples. Every summer, an elaborate, symphonic outdoor drama titled "The Lost Colony" is staged nightly at Fort Raleigh. This play is more than 50 years old, which makes it the longest running theatrical production in America.

The restaurants in and around Nags Head and the Outer Banks are

Interspersed with 15 freshwater lagoons and marsh creeks, Bald Head Island may be architect George Cobb's crowning achievement.

insouciant affairs where, even for dinner, people wear sandals and shorts. Hanging plants, paper placemats illustrated with maps and sea shells, and menus featuring fried fish and hush puppies predominate. There are some standouts, however, in Nags Head, Windmill Point and the nearby town of Manteo, and in most cases the prices are as agreeable as the food.

As for golf, the Outer Banks doesn't have the notoriety of its neighbors in the Sandhills and the Smoky Mountains. That's a pity, for the Outer Banks has redefined the game on its own terms. Carved from the windswept dunes, the courses here are devoid of trees; after all, this spit of land is a prime target for hurricanes rolling in across the Eastern Seaboard. With only the low, hardy vegetation with which to contend— as well as a sprinkling of requisite bunkers and water hazards—golfers are left to go head-to-head with the wind. It is this singular challenge, coupled with the intimate charm and breathtaking beauty, that leaves you to believe that this is the way golf was meant to be played.

For More Information

Cape Fear Coast Convention and Visitors Bureau, P.O. Box 266, Wilmington, NC 28402; (800) 222-4757 or (910) 341-4030. For golf information in the Wilmington area, call Tee Times of Wilmington, (800) 447-0450. For information on the Outer Banks, contact the Chamber of Commerce, P.O. Box 1757, Kill Devil Hills, NC 27948; (919) 441-8144.

THE RESORTS IN DEPTH

Bald Head Island

"The Timeless Appeal of a Natural Masterpiece"

Unbound by bridges, and the accompanying crowds, Bald Head Island may be the closest thing to pure bliss in the natural world. There are no cars, no fast food haunts, and no timeshares. There's not much noise to speak of, save for the frequent cry of a seabird or the hushed drone of a shrimp boat passing by. Rather, it's serenity and quietness and the being-at-one-with-nature thing.

Bald Head Island is the southernmost point along the North Carolina coast and a fitting finale – or opening, depending on your direction – to the state's magnificent string of barrier islands and capes. As part of the charming and historic Cape Fear region, the island is surprisingly close for a world that seems so distantly removed.

The mainland base for Bald Head is the quaint coastal town of Southport, where the private passenger ferry allows guests to toss their cares and worries overboard for the 15-minute ride to Shangri-La. By the time you arrive, your brain has downloaded sufficiently for the encounter with this lush 2,000-acre masterpiece of nature.

Such resort destinations are rare nowadays, but Bald Head Island is certainly no newcomer as a coastal retreat. On the contrary, it has a colorful past, full of history and legend.

Off the tip of the island are the Frying Pan Shoals, where, as legend has it, pirates would plant false beacons to draw unwary ships onto the shoals where they would be plundered. Of course, you may have heard that story about every barrier island on the North Carolina coast. In reality, much of Bald Head's character has evolved from its more heroic turn-of-the-century days as a beacon to those seeking safer waters. The U.S. Life Saving Service was once based here, and the Boat House remains as testimony to the days when crews would roll out the surf boats in times of crisis.

In 1903, Captain Charlie Swan moved to the island as keeper of the Cape Fear Lighthouse. The three homes on the South Beach, known affectionately as Captain Charlie's Station, provide a vivid picture of the lifestyle he and his family enjoyed. But the landmark bearing the greatest significance is Old Baldy. Built in 1817, it is North Carolina's oldest lighthouse and now stands as the island's only high-rise. Take that, Myrtle Beach.

The primeval beauty of Bald Head Island endures much as it has for

An outstanding design by Rees Jones, The Emerald, in New Bern, has been the site of several regional and local tournaments.

The 10th green at Nags Head Golf Links.

centuries. Its 14 miles of unspoiled beach remains wide, gently sloping and inviting—yes, yours may be the only footprints in the sand, even in the summer—and a vast maritime forest provides a sanctuary for a variety of wildlife and vegetation, which thrive in the semitropical climate. The East Beach is a major spawning ground for loggerhead turtles.

So what *is* there to do when the affinity for seclusion wears thin? Well, tennis buffs and anglers will feel just as accommodated as shell collectors and porch rockers. And if you don't play golf during your sojourn to Bald Head Island, you've missed the proverbial boat.

Bald Head offers an outstanding George Cobb layout that plays 6,855 yards and is as tough as a loggerhead's shell. The course winds through the maritime forest and is interspersed with 15 freshwater lagoons and marsh creeks. The highlight, though, is the magnificent par-three 16th that plays out to a green set hard against the Atlantic. This is a perfectly wonderful spot for a golf course, and Cobb certainly did the site justice. Of all of his work throughout the Carolinas, both coastal and inland, Bald Head Island may be Cobb's crowning achievement.

Despite its unconventional, yet welcome mode of transportation around the island—who wants a car when you can wheel around in a golf cart?—Bald Head also offers all the recreational trappings of a major resort destination. Besides its four all-weather tennis courts and a seemingly endless array of ponds for wetting a line, there's a 25-meter swimming pool, two croquet courts, three restaurants, a marina, and seasonal children's activities.

But for those whose brain waves are still on "Do Not Disturb," there's the serenity of bird watching or the 20-minute hike around the Bald Head Island Conservancy's nature trail, or biking along the island's three miles of paved paths. Better yet, take the bikes to the beach at dawn, watch the sun come up over the shoals, and immerse yourself in the smells, the sights and, particularly, the sounds of solitude.

The Village at Nags Head
"A Bit Of The Old Country On The Outer Banks"

It is pure Scotland, save perhaps for the heather and a lone piper at dusk. While every third or fourth new golf course in the U.S. lays claim to some semblance of Scottish-style design elements, Nags Head Golf Links is the genuine article.

It's true. These other courses that boast a similarity to golf in the game's birthplace are dreadfully contrived, with studied mounding and imported plantings and pot bunkers that look as natural as bowls filled with sugar. But Nags Head, located within The Village at Nags Head community on the desolate, wind-whipped Outer Banks, is a spread on which Old Tom Morris would have been downright cozy.

This course was nothing but a humongous sand dune before North Carolina architect Bob Moore transformed it into a bit of Firth of Forth. His was not a taxing endeavor. In fact, his genius with this course lay in leaving well enough alone. He didn't mess with Mother Nature.

True to Scottish form, the course offers a wonderfully scrubby, untamed, treeless terrain with shaggy-lipped pot bunkers that appear to have been more the handiwork of burrowing animals than man. The rough is sandy, wind-swept wasteland composed of love grass, sea oats, purple and yellow wildflowers and what the locals call "miracle bushes"—low, fat hedge-like growths that sprout with abandon. (It is considered nothing less than divine intervention when anything green survives in this region, hence the name of said fauna.)

Several of the holes skirt the vast, churning Roanoke Sound, so shallow that you can walk through it to neighboring islands. The fiendishly tight fairways twist and wind their way through wasteland like corkscrews. On several holes the rough cuts across the fairways in strategic locations; bottlenecks and blind shots abound. This is a cerebral test; forget about muscle, for it will do you no good. What counts are those "little gray cells," to borrow a phrase from a famed Agatha Christie detective. And indeed, this layout can be rather a mystery.

The ninth and 18th holes at Nags Head finish dramatically alongside the sea.

Nags Head Golf Links measures but 5,717 from the white tees (6,126 from the tips), but the wind more than compensates for the minimal length on this par-71. The entire disposition of this course changes from hour to hour, depending on which way the ever-robust gale is blowing. A sudden wallop of wind from the Southeast can turn a string of holes into a fire-breathing dragon. A gust from the Northeast can convert the same stretch into an eager-to-please lap dog. If any course in America exhibits

radical Jekyll-and-Hyde tendencies, it's Nags Head.

Beware the dogleg-left, par-4 seventh hole, whose green is a vortex of nasty crosswinds. Of the five par-3s, the 15th is the meanest. At 221 yards from the tips and 202 yards from the regular tees, the hole offers sand dunes to the right and a pond and marsh grass in front of the green. The par-five 18th is truly a grand finale. Long and scenic, it snakes treacherously along the sound, where windsails bob and waft, and tapers into a bottleneck that has to be one of the tightest squeezes in golf.

To rent a home at The Village—two hotels and a number of condominiums are still in the works—is to enter an ultra-cool refuge of pastels and ceiling fans. The decor is effortlessly tasteful. The social hub of The Village is the Beach Club, a sprawling structure overlooking the Atlantic where festivities evolve around such indigenous feasts as pig picking's, chicken sticken's, oyster roasts and clambakes. And wildlife has not been evicted in favor of progress at The Village. Amazingly tame deer graze around the houses, and foxes scramble through the brush. It isn't at all unusual to see a mallard dozing poolside at the Beach Club.

The Village at Nags Head has a light, airy restaurant fittingly called the Links Room, which renders wide vistas of the golf course and the sound. Among the delectable entrees are scallops with citrus sauce and blackened pork tenderloin. The focal point of this restaurant is a stunning fireplace, the unpolished stones of which were culled from farmland in the North Carolina mountains. With its rough-cedar paneling, intimate bar and inviting fireplace, the Links Room is an ideal setting in which to savor an *apres*-golf dram and ponder the birdies that got away.

But the 19th Hole ritual at The Village would be incomplete without a visit to the lookout tower atop the clubhouse, where there awaits an astonishingly Scottish panorama. Your imagination can paint in the heather and lone piper.

ALSO IN THE AREA

Beau Rivage Plantation
A dramatically rolling course with elevation changes of up to 70 feet. Well-treed with oak and pines; bermuda fairways and bentgrass greens.

Belvedere Plantation G. & C.C.
Course is located on the Intracoastal Waterway and is built through pine trees with rolling fairways, elevated greens and an abundance of water. Noted for its excellent conditioning.

Brandywine Bay C.C.
Bruce Devlin designed this challenging daily-fee course near Morehead City. Lots of water here.

The Cape G. & R. C.
Challenging course situated between the Atlantic Ocean and the Cape Fear River. Tall pines, narrow fairways, well-bunkered greens and 16 water holes. Hole Nos. 15 and 17 share a green.

Duck Woods C.C.
Relatively short Ellis Maples course in the midst of pines, hardwood and marshland in Kitty Hawk. Lots of water hazards. Course is private from July through Labor Day, semi-private remainder of year.

Echo Farms G. & C.C.
Formerly a dairy farm, this course is cut through a dense stand of pines on the front side. It's more open on the back nine, with water coming into play on five holes.

The Emerald G.C.
Excellent Rees Jones design that's part of a residential community being developed by Weyerhauser. Set among tall pines with 32 acres of lakes, but no forced carries. Fairly flat and well-bunkered. Plays 6,924 yards from the tips, but is eminently playable. Formerly known as Greenbrier.

North Shore C.C.
Championship course bordering the Intracoastal Waterway near Sneads Ferry. A mix of holes wind through marshland areas and tall pines with gentle mounding and numerous creeks and ponds.

Olde Point G. & C.C.
Scenic, gently rolling terrain with large bentgrass greens and water in play on 14 holes. Course plays 6,913 yards and runs through a semi-private community.

Sea Scape G.C.
Designed by 1959 Masters champion Art Wall, this short course near Kitty Hawk offers magnificent views of the ocean. A Scottish-style links design that's buffeted by the elements. Greens are bentgrass. Fees go as low as $18 in off-season.

Silver Creek G.C.
A Gene Hamm course located south of New Bern near the coast. Layout features undulating fairways and greens, an abundance of bunkers and water on 11 holes.

Topsail Greens G.C.
A shotmaker's course designed by Russell Birney with small greens and pine trees. Water comes into play on more than half of the holes on this 6,331-yard layout. With fees and cart ranging from $22 to $29, this is a good value.

MYRTLE

Designed by an amateur course architect, Tidewater is inarguably the finest new course in the entire Grand Strand area. Note how architect Ken Tomlinson built several "compartments" within this marshside par-3 green to demand accuracy off the tee while still building a green large enough to withstand the heavy golf traffic that visits the Grand Strand.

BEACH

Myrtle Beach

The Complete List of Courses Open to the Public

Location	Course	Address
Calabash	**Marsh Harbour G.L.	201 Marsh Harbour Rd.
Conway	*Wild Wing Plantation—	
	Hummingbird Course	585 100 St.
	Avocet Course	585 100 St.
	Wood Stork Course	585 100 St.
	*The Witch	1900 Highway 544
Little River	Cypress Bay	Highway 17 N.
	Eastport G.C.	Highway 17 N.
	**Heather Glen G. L.	Highway 17 N.
Longs	River Hills G. & C.C.	P.O. Box 1049
	Buck Creek G.P.	Highway 9
	Colonial Charters	301 Charter Dr.
Murrells Inlet	**Long Bay Club	Highway 9
Myrtle Beach	Blackmoor Club	Highway 7070
	**Arcadian Shores G.C.	701 Hilton Rd.
	Burning Ridge—	
	East Course	Highway 501 W.
	West Course	Highway 501 W.
	Deer Track G. & C.C.—	
	North Course	Highway 17 S.
	South Course	Highway 17 S.
	**Dunes G. & C.C.	9000 W. Ocean Blvd.
	Heron Pointe G.C.	6980 Blue Heron Blvd.
	Island Green G.C. (27)	P.O. Box 4747
	Legends—	
	Heathland	P.O. Box 2038
	**Moorland	P.O. Box 2038
	Parkland	P.O. Box 2038
	Myrtle Beach National—	
	North Course	807 Palmetta Dr.
	South Course	807 Palmetta Dr.
	West Course	807 Palmetta Dr.
	Myrtlewood G.C.—	
	Pine Hills Course	Highway 17 Bypass
	Palmetto Course	Highway 17 Bypass
	Pine Lakes Int. G.C.	5803 Woodside Ave.
	Quail Creek G,C.	Highway 501
	Raccoon Run	8950 Highway 7070
	River Oaks G.C. (27)	3400 Highway 501 W.
	Waterway Hills (27)	9731 Highway 17 N.
N. Myrtle Beach	Azalea Sands G.C.	Highway 17

* Recommended Course ** Highly Recommended

Rating/Slope: Men	Women	Par	Cost	Phone
na/134	—	71	High	(803) 249-3449
70.0/123	69.5/123	72	Very High	(803) 347-9464
—	69.5/121	72	Very High	(803) 347-9464
71.8/117	—	72	Very High	(803) 347-9464
na/133	—	72	High	(803) 347-2706
70.0/119	70.2/120	72	Low	(803) 249-1025
na/116	—	70	Moderate	(803) 249-3997
70.6/126	69.3/117	72	High	(800) 868-4536
na/138	—	72	High	(803) 399-2100
69.6/126	67.5/117	72	Moderate	(803) 399-2660
69.8/122	72.0/122	72	Moderate	(803) 399-4653
72.1/130	72.1/127	72	Very High	(803) 249-5510
na/126	—	72	High	(803) 650-5555
71/131	69.9/117	72	High	(803) 449-5217
69.7/119	65.4/111	72	Moderate	(803) 347-0538
69.4/114	66.5/118	72	Moderate	(803) 347-0538
70.8/121	70.4/120	72	Moderate	(803) 650-2146
69.3/119	70.5/119	71	Moderate	(803) 650-2146
71.5/130	70.8/127	72	Very High	(803) 449-5914
69.4/119	69.2/121	72	Moderate	(803) 650-6663
67.3/111	67.4/118	72	High	(803) 650-2186
69.0/121	—	72	High	(803) 236-9318
70.9/123	—	72	High	(803) 236-9318
70.6/123	—	72	High	(803) 236-9318
68.8/109	67.6/113	72	Moderate	(803) 448-2308
69.1/118	66.5/109	72	Moderate	(803) 448-2308
68.9/113	68.3/109	72	Moderate	(803) 448-2308
68.3/113	67.7/111	72	Moderate	(803) 449-5134
70.6/118	70.1/117	72	Moderate	(803) 449-5134
71.0/129	69.6/120	71	Very High	(803) 449-6459
69.7/113	66.5/106	72	Moderate	(803) 347-0549
71.0/116	69.5/109	73	Moderate	(803) 650-2644
69.7/125	68.1/118	72	Moderate	(803) 263-2222
71.2/126	67.5/127	72	Moderate	(803) 449-6488
69.5/116	70.0/119	72	Low	(803) 272-6191

Myrtle Beach

The Complete List of Courses Open to the Public

Location	Course	Address
N. Myrtle Beach	Bay Tree G. Pl.—	
	*Gold Course	P.O. Box 240
	*Green Course	P.O. Box 240
	Silver Course	P.O. Box 240
	Beachwood G.C.	1520 Highway 17 N.
	Eagle Nest G.C.	Highway 17 N.
	*Gator Hole G.C.	7th Ave. Highway 17
	Myrtle West G.C.	Highway 9
	**Oyster Bay G.L.	P.O. Box 65
	Possum Trot G.C.	Possum Trot Rd.
	*Surf G. & B.C.	1701 Springland Ln.
	**Tidewater	4901 Little River Neck Rd.
Pawleys Island	Litchfield C.C.—	
	The Club Course	P.O. Box 379
	River Club	P.O. Box 379
	Willbrook Pl.	P.O. Box 379
	The Heritage Club	Highway 17 S.
	Sea Gull G.C.	Highway 17 S.
Surfside	Indian Wells G.C.	Highway 17
Surfside Beach	Indigo Creek G.C.	Highway 17 Bypass
Calabash, NC	Carolina Shores G.C.	99 Carolina Shores Dr.
	Sandpiper Bay G. & C.C.	6660 Sandpiper Bay Dr.
Holden Beach, NC	*Lockwood G.L.	100 Clubhouse Dr.
Ocean Isle, NC	Brick Landing	44 Windsong Dr.
	Lion's Paw G.C.	351 Ocean Ridge Pkwy. S.W.
Southport, NC	*The Gauntlet G. & C.C.	Highway 211
Sunset Beach, NC	*The Pearl—	
	East Course	1300 Pearl Blvd.
	West Course	1300 Pearl Blvd.
	**Sea Trail Plantation—	
	Byrd Course	211 Clubhouse Rd.
	Jones Course	211 Clubhouse Rd.
	Maples Course	211 Clubhouse Rd.

* Recommended Course ** Highly Recommended

MYRTLE BEACH, S.C., MAY BE THE GREATEST PLACE TO PLAY GOLF in the world. It certainly is the most generous, offering the most value for the dollar. While most aspects of a successful golfing destination are fairly obvious—climate, proximity to the sea or scenery, great golf, an ample

Rating/Slope: Men	Women	Par	Cost	Phone
71.5/126	70.8/118	72	Moderate	(803) 249-1487
71.0/128	70.0/117	72	Moderate	(803) 249-1487
70.3/122	70.6/116	72	Moderate	(803) 249-1487
68.8/117	67.6/111	72	Moderate	(803) 272-6168
70.4/116	69.4/117	72	Moderate	(803) 249-1449
66.3/107	65.4/106	70	High	(803) 249-3543
69.1/118	67.6/113	72	High	(803) 249-3462
72.4/134	71.9/126	71	Very High	(803) 272-6399
69.7/118	70.8/122	72	Moderate	(803) 373-5341
71.2/126	67.5/127	72	Very High	(803) 249-1524
68.8/115	68.2/113	72	Very High	(803) 249-3829
70.6/119	70.8/119	72	Moderate	(803) 237-3411
69.9/119	67.7/120	72	Moderate	(803) 237-3411
68.6/117	67.7/118	72	High	(803) 237-3411
na/137	—	71	High	(803) 237-3424
69.0/116	68.3/113	72	Moderate	(803) 448-5931
70.0/123	68.2/118	72	Moderate	(803) 651-1505
70.0/120	69.2/120	72	High	(803) 650-0081
69.4/114	66.5/118	72	Moderate	(919) 579-2181
70.8/128	69.8/121	71	Moderate	(919) 579-9120
70.7/129	70.0/121	72	High	(919) 842-5666
69.4/132	67.8/114	72	Moderate	(919) 754-4373
71.6/130	69.1/118	71	Moderate	(919) 579-1801
71.3/132	69.7/119	72	High	(800) 247-4806
70.8/127	70.2/121	72	High	(919) 579-8132
71.0/129	69.6/120	72	High	(919) 579-8132
70.4/126	67.9/111	72	High	(919) 579-4350
70.4/126	68.5/115	72	High	(919) 579-4350
70.1/117	68.5/108	72	High	(919) 579-4350

supply of rooms, a good airport and convention center, and a variety of restaurants and activities for non-golfers—other factors like pricing and marketing are the underlying keys to the success of any resort destination. There are places with better resorts, better airports, and better convention

The opening of the Oyster Bay (pictured above) and Marsh Harbour courses, both designed by Dan Maples, paved the way for the renaissance of Myrtle Beach golf in the 1980s.

facilities, but collectively and on every other count, Myrtle Beach outstrips the competition hands down.

Here's the facts: There are presently 70,000 hotel rooms on the "Grand Strand;" there will be about 100 golf courses by the year 2000 (at least 20 of which are superior and three that have been chosen "Best New Public Course of the Year" in the past 10 years by *Golf Digest*). You can make reservations and tee times in advance by calling Golf Holiday at (800) 845-4653, stay at a choice of reasonably priced or even inexpensively priced hotels, motels or condominiums, and play most all of the courses. There is a wonderful beach on the Atlantic with warm water temperatures (the Brits and Canadians will swim in November, no problem), an amusement park pavilion, big shopping malls, hundreds of restaurants, gigantic fantasy-land miniature golf courses, a major golf instruction center, the largest amateur golf tournament in the world, and a major convention center. And the weather? There are maybe 10 days a year when you can't play golf; maybe another 20 when you might not want to.

The Grand Strand, a sandy spit of land about 60 miles long, was originally an Indian fishing ground and is still ideally suited for fishing with deep sea, lake and river fishing all natural to the area. The region occupies a peninsula known

Above: One of the most ambitious projects ever undertaken in Myrtle Beach, the Legends complex was developed by Larry Young, who was also responsible for Marsh Harbour and Oyster Bay. It includes three stellar courses. Pictured above are the wind-swept Heathland, and the undulating, heavily bunkered Moorland course. Above right: The Witch, designed by Dan Maples.

as the Waccamaw Neck. Bordered on the east by a 60-mile-long crescent-shaped coastline, and on the west by the Waccamaw River, it is 12 miles wide at the North Carolina state line and, at its widest, 14 miles from the lowlands of Conway, S.C. to Myrtle Beach. In many of the present developments, such as Litchfield Plantation, the neck is narrow enough that the properties stretch from the river on one side to the Atlantic on the other.

This neck has seen more development in the last 50 years than any other area along the Southeastern Seaboard and, during the incredible growth of the 1980s, perhaps more than any remotely comparable stretch of land anywhere including Orlando, Fla. The Grand Strand now stretches from Pawleys Island near Georgetown at the southern tip of the sand spit to the end of the giant sandbar in North Carolina, past the beach side of Calabash, N.C. (home of some of the area's finest little seafood houses) and on toward Wilmington. There's seemingly no end in sight in either direction.

The bottom line is still the same: Myrtle Beach has the greatest golf—in terms of quality and quantity—at the best monetary value to be found anywhere. The golf package rates are so good that it might be less expensive to come to the Beach than to stay home. Try a week of intravenous dimple-chasing, 36 holes a day with never the same hole played twice. Sample a different restaurant every night, jog on the beach in the morning and share in the incredible energy that millions of visitors discover each year. In Myrtle Beach, the golfer is the master of this very unique, very special universe.

Getting There

Airline service to the Myrtle Beach Jetport is offered by USAir, American Airlines and Atlantic Southeast Airlines (Delta's regional commuter). The jetport offers a full selection of car rental, taxi and limousine services. The Grand Strand Airport in North Myrtle Beach caters to private aircraft with full service and general aviation facilities. By car, U.S. Routes 17 and 501 and S.C. Route 9 provide direct access to the Grand Strand from Interstate Highways 95 and 20. Amtrak service to the Grand Strand is available through a terminal in Florence, S.C., and buses connect with Amtrak for the 70-mile drive to Myrtle Beach.

Weather

The semi-tropical climate enjoyed in the Myrtle Beach area allows for outdoor activity year-round, save perhaps for ocean swimming during the winter months when the water temperature dips into the high 40s. Average high temperatures range from 75 degrees in the spring (March-May) and fall (September/November), to 88 degrees in the summer (June-August) and 57 degrees in the winter (December-February). Myrtle Beach averages about 77 days of rain per year and 215 days of sunshine annually.

Activities

Obviously, the biggest draws are golf and the beach. But fishing should also rank highly as well. Whether you cast your line from the surf, a public pier or a charter boat, you'll probably wind up with a pretty good catch. Surf fishing is permitted all along the beach, and there are public piers at Garden City, Surfside, Second Avenue, Myrtle Beach State Park, Windy Hill, Kits, Crescent Beach, Tilghman Beach, Cherry Grove and Springmaid. Charter boats are available at marinas up and down the Grand Strand, and even at the height of the season you'll be able to book a trip without much difficulty. Depending on the season, your haul may include croaker, bluefish, flounder, spot, pompano, black sea bass, or whiting. One other note about Grand Strand water sports: the scuba diving here is remarkable. Several shipwrecks located off the coast offer endless appeal to the inquisitive diver. The fishing is also outstanding around this wreckage. When you tire of all this activity, a nice diversion is a stroll along the Myrtle Beach boardwalk, lined with all sorts of amusements and ideal for a window-shopping stroll. Another thing to remember about the Grand Strand: The tone here is of a family-oriented resort, with almost as much attention paid to children's needs as to those of adults. Many lodging providers offer activity programs and playgrounds with supervision, and nearly all have babysitter lists for parents who want to enjoy the Grand Strand's diverse nightlife.

Attractions

For family entertainment, the first stop is The Pavilion Amusement Park, with activities for all ages including thrill and kiddie rides, video games, a teen nightclub, specialty shops, antique cars and sidewalk cafes. Nearby is the Guinness Hall of World Records, Ripley's Believe It Or Not Museum, and Myrtle Beach National Wax Museum. There's also Myrtle Beach Grand Prix, for auto-maniacs both young and old, in two locations on the Strand; and Myrtle Waves Water Park, with 17 rides and attractions for all ages, open from May through Labor Day. When you've had enough of the more raucous amusements, it's time to head out of town. South of Myrtle Beach is Murrell's Inlet, a picturesque fishing village with some of the finest seafood restaurants on the Strand. Further south is Brookgreen

Gary Player's lone Grand Strand course is the short but tricky Blackmoor Club.

Long Bay, one of the Grand Strand's most highly-regarded layouts, is one of only two by Jack Nicklaus in the area.

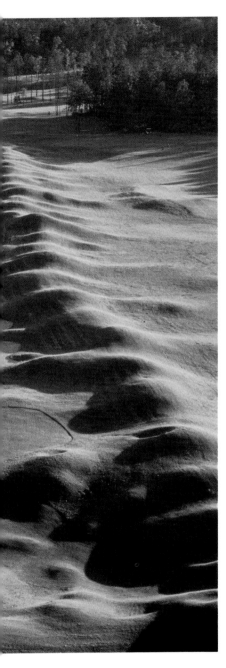

Gardens, the world's largest sculpture garden, set among 9,000 beautifully landscaped acres that include a wildlife park, an aviary, a cypress swamp, nature trails, and an education center. Just across the highway is Huntington Beach State Park, a 2,500-acre former estate that includes the Moorish-style castle "Atalaya," once the home of the Huntington family. Continue a little further south and you'll come to Pawleys Island, the great old summer resort with weathered cottages nestled among groves of oleander and oak trees. This is where the famous rope hammocks have been handmade since the 1800s. Should you need a little pick-me-up after a full day of touring, head back into town for a great musical show. The Carolina Opry and The Dixie Jubilee are both outstanding entertainment values for the entire family, as is the Dixie Stampede, a rollicking dinner attraction that is partly owned by singer Dolly Parton.

Shopping

The Grand Strand is served by many fine shopping centers, malls, and outlet complexes. Myrtle Square Mall (71 stores and restaurants) and Briarcliffe Mall (100 specialty shops and department stores) are among the largest; one of the newest and most popular complexes is Barefoot Landing , with 100 retail and outlet stores, a dozen restaurants, and a 40-foot carousel in an attractive waterfront setting. For outlet shopping, little can compare with Waccamaw Pottery and Outlet Park on U.S. 501, a sprawling maze of 50 outlet stores including the main store that contains three miles of shelves stocked with china, glassware, wicker, brass, and pewter. Across the street is the Hathaway Factory Outlet with menswear by Christian Dior and Ralph Lauren and women's wear by White Stag and Geoffrey Beene, among others. The best location for specialty shopping is the Hammock Shops at Pawleys Island, a beautiful complex of 17 boutiques and gift shops, including a shop where the Pawleys Island hammocks are made before your eyes.

Popular Dining Options

At first, you may think that the Grand Strand offers nothing but fast food and Calabash Seafood houses (where heaping portions of breaded, deep-fried seafood items are served buffet-style). Actually, the Myrtle Beach area offers some outstanding restaurants with Continental and classic American cuisine. Among the best: *Planter's Back Porch* in Murrell's Inlet, reminiscent of the 19th-century Southern plantation with outstanding fresh seafood dishes; *Rice Planter's Restaurant*, with fresh seafood, steaks, quail, and homemade bread and pecan pie in a homey setting; and *Pawleys Island Inn Restaurant and Bar*, with four dining rooms in an Antebellum-style inn serving outstanding local seafood dishes and homemade desserts. Other restaurants of note include *Slug's Choice* in Myrtle Beach, a popular spot with outstanding prime rib and steaks, fresh local seafood, and a lounge that overlooks the Intracoastal Waterway; *Sea Captain's House*, a picturesque restaurant with nautical decor and sweeping ocean views and local seafood dishes, locations at Ocean Boulevard and in Murrell's Inlet; and *Southern Suppers*, a farmhouse filled with country primitive art and offering a seafood buffet as well as down-home Southern specialties like country-fried steak, fried chicken, and country ham with red-eye gravy and grits.

For More Information

The Myrtle Beach Chamber of Commerce, 1301 North Kings Highway, P.O. Box 2115, Myrtle Beach, SC 29578-2115, (800) 356-3016 or (803) 626-7444. Also, the Myrtle Beach Area Convention Bureau, 710 21st Avenue North, Hampton Park Suite J, Myrtle Beach, SC 29577, (803) 448-1629.

THE RESORTS IN DEPTH

Sea Trail Plantation
"Pure Golf at The Strand's Only True Resort"

It is almost inconceivable that, along the entire 60-odd miles of the Grand Strand, there is only one true golf resort destination. That distinction goes to Sea Trail Plantation, and it is maintaining its singular presence very well, thank you.

Sea Trail is a resort and residential community that encompasses more than 2,000 acres in Sunset Beach, N.C., a largely rural area just across the South Carolina state line. It's an area of remarkable beauty; clear, natural lakes and the Calabash River Creek flow through Sea Trail's interior, which is dense with forests of stately oaks, cypress longleaf pines and holly, and large, rolling sandy ridges. Wildlife runs rampant throughout the plantation and around its perimeter, which is formed by the Atlantic Ocean and its inland salt marshes, and the Intracoastal Waterway. It's a peaceful respite from the bustle of the Grand Strand, yet close enough (20-30 minutes to the heart of Myrtle Beach) to not be an inconvenience.

The resort operations at Sea Trail are managed by Clarion, and the package that's offered is strong enough to be voted Clarion's Inn of the Year for 1991 by its parent company, Choice Hotels International. Accommodations consist of villas and townhomes of one to four bedrooms in a variety of settings. All are fully furnished and offer screened porches and private balconies that overlook the golf fairways or the Calabash River Creek. There are two clubhouses, each with a restaurant and lounge, and an activities center with lighted tennis courts, swimming pools and a health and fitness center. Sunset Beach is a short drive away, across the Intracoastal Waterway.

But if you come to Sea Trail, on holiday or on a more permanent basis, chances are you've come for the golf. The 54-hole rotation at Sea Trail rivals anything on the Grand Strand for variety, quality and beauty. And few properties along the Southeastern Coast can match Sea Trail's trio of designers: Dan Maples, Rees Jones and Willard Byrd.

Dan Maples, whose roots in golf course design and construction reach back to the 19th century, has certainly created more prolific courses in the area than his 18-hole layout at Sea Trail. His Oyster Bay and Marsh Harbour courses are both ranked among the "Top 25 Public Courses in America" by *Golf Digest*; in fact, Oyster Bay is located within the boundaries of Sea Trail Plantation. But Maples' Sea Trail course, opened in 1985, is a sleeper, a subtle stroke of brilliance in a magnificent setting.

**Above: The Heather Glen Golf Club, an acclaimed course designed by Willard Byrd.
Below left: The finishing hole on The Pearl's West Course.**

It winds along the lakes, creeks and marshes of the plantation, playing 6,761 yards from the blue tees and 6,334 yards from the regular markers, with par at 72. The forests of twisted oaks and towering Carolina pines define each hole, and Maples' imaginative bunkering - ranging from deep greenside traps to a nearly 400-yard waste bunker at the 15th hole - lends enormous character to the design. The tight fairways and large bentgrass greens are typically well-maintained.

Rees Jones opened his course at Sea Trail in the spring of 1990 with a combination of traditional and modern elements. The fairways are wide,

In addition to Willard Byrd and Dan Maples courses, Sea Trail (pictured above) is home to an excellent course by Rees Jones. Jones cut his teeth in the Myrtle Beach area, collaborating with his father Robert Trent Jones on the Waterway Hills course, and later adding to his considerable reputation with the sublime Arcadian Shores and the underrated Gator Hole course.

the greens are elevated, and there's an abundance of mounds, swales and pot bunkers. But water also comes into play on 11 holes, and in several instances, its challenge is most evident around the greens. There's even a bit of bulkheading, most notably at the excellent par-3 fifth that requires 189 yards of carry from the tips. Measuring 6,761 yards from the blue tees and 6,334 from the whites, the Jones course has been lauded throughout

the Grand Strand for its conditioning and design values.

Following on the heels of the Jones course was the 18-hole course designed by Willard Byrd, which opened in the fall of 1990. Byrd is no stranger to the Carolina Lowcountry—he has designed no less than 15 courses in the Myrtle Beach area and on Hilton Head Island—and his design at Sea Trail is quintessential Byrd. Measuring 6,750 yards from the tips and just 6,263 yards from the regular markers, the course rambles through the forests and around several man-made lakes with sprawling fairway bunkers (mostly directional) and large, bentgrass greens. Like many of Byrd's designs, this course is highly playable from the forward tees while offering a good challenge from the championship markers.

Guests at Sea Trail are afforded preferred tee times and rates at the resort's three courses. But like many of the other hotel properties along the Grand Strand, guests have access to some of the area's other fine courses through a variety of special packages. Of special note is the Sea Trail Exclusive Package, which offers villa accommodations, breakfast, and daily green fees on the three Sea Trail courses with free replays on a space available basis (daily rates from $35, weekly rates from $225), and the Preferred Courses Package, which includes green fees with no surcharges at 56 area courses (daily rates from $56, weekly from $351).

It's a best-of-both-worlds scenario, if you will. Sea Trail is close enough to the endless array of amenities and activities of the Grand Strand, while affording its guests the luxury of a private, secluded golf environment. For those seeking the convenience of a self-contained resort destination, Sea

Trail's the only game in town. And when you're playing alone, it's pretty hard to lose.

Arcadian Shores G.C.

Gorgeous track with an excellent early Rees Jones design. Bentgrass greens, 64 bunkers, and several natural lakes make this one of the area's most aesthetically pleasing courses. Very well maintained year-round. Course has been honored by major golf publications as one of the top 100 in the country.

Azalea Sands G.C.

Well manicured course with large greens, an abundance of trees and bunkers, and strategically placed lakes. Walking is permitted during certain times of the year.

Bay Tree Golf Plantation

Gold Course gained national attention as host site of the 1977 LPGA Championship. Green Course, nicknamed the "Green Monster," hosts one of the PGA's qualifying schools; in 1975, Danny Edwards earned his Tour card with a four-round total of 13-over par. Silver Course is the members' favorite, more forgiving than the other two, but a challenge nevertheless. All three courses have significant undulations in their Bermuda greens.

Beachwood G.C.

Enjoyable and highly playable course that's kept in fine condition year-round. Hosted the 1989 Carolinas Open and annually hosts the Carolinas PGA Seniors Championship.

Blackmoor G.C.

Located in Longwood Plantation along the Waccamaw River, this playable course offers gently rolling terrain. It's Player's first design in the Grand Strand area and, like many of his other designs, aesthetics are placed at a higher premium than challenge.

Brick Landing Plantation

Winds along the Intracoastal Waterway through hardwood forests and scenic saltwater marshes. Wind presents the biggest challenge here.

Brunswick Plantation & G.L.
New Willard Byrd design set in the heart of a 600-acre residential plantation. Front nine mixes tree-lined fairways, strategic bunkering and water hazards with three open, Scottish-style holes. Back nine is more demanding with thick woodlands and two difficult par-threes. Greens are quick Penncross bentgrass.

Buck Creek Golf Plantation
Tucked among towering hardwoods along the Waccamaw River, this is a very scenic course. Toughest rotation is Cypress/Tupelo.

Burning Ridge G.C.
Both courses offer gently rolling fairways, towering trees and numerous lakes. East Course offers generous landing areas off the tee and well-protected greens. West Course has water on virtually every hole, but the fairways are wide and the greens are large.

Carolina Shores G.C.
A popular, challenging course with numerous fairway mounds, large lakes, and 96 sand bunkers. Narrow fairways wind through forests of hardwoods and pines, and the Bermuda greens are large.

Colonial Charters G.C.
Host site of numerous tournaments, this course is built on 185 acres of Carolina pines interlaced with dogwoods, holly and native hardwoods. Hosed, among other tournaments, the 1993 NCAA Big South Conference Championships. Also home to the "Swing's The Thing" golf school.

Cypress Bay G.C.
Well-maintained course nestled among the cypress and pines in Little River. Course features its own landing strip.

Deer Track Golf Resort
Longer North Course offers wide tree-lined fairways, elevated bentgrass greens and picturesque surroundings. South Course is a more modern design with sculpted bunkering, dramatically rolling bentgrass greens and numerous lakes and ponds. Head professional is Gary Schaal, the current president of the PGA of America.

The Dunes Golf & Beach Club

A legendary course, having been ranked among the top 100 courses in the U.S. The 13th hole ranks as one of the world's great par-fives, an uphill dogleg-right that has allegedly has been reached in two by only one man, Mike Souchak. The Dunes has hosted the U.S. Women's Open and will host the 1996 U.S. Senior Open.. A "must-play" on the Grand Strand, provided you stay at a hotel that has guest privileges.

This par-5 at The River Club, while retaining the heroic route for the master golfer, has an alternative route, away from the water, offering a safe par opportunity for the apprentice.

Eagles Nest G.C.

A long and challenging, well-maintained layout. Numerous lakes and tree-lined fairways. Last three holes provide one of the Grand Strand's tougher finishes.

Eastport G.C.

Short, finesse course with natural undulating terrain and elevated, bentgrass greens. Numerous pot bunkers and waste areas. Course offers several views of the Intracoastal Waterway.

Gator Hole G.C.

Excellent Rees Jones course with rolling hills, sand dunes, moss-laden oaks, and natural marshlands. Accuracy is paramount to good scoring. Course is well-maintained and offers six fine par-threes. A sleeper, and an excellent value as well.

The Gauntlet G. & C.C.

Challenging P.B. Dye design set on 200 acres of marsh, woodlands and lakes in St. James Plantation. Plays along the Intracoastal Waterway. Course rating of 75.0 from the tips; slope ratings are among the highest on the Grand Strand.

Heather Glen G.L.

A heralded course cited by *Golf Digest* as the "Best New Public Course in America" in 1987. Built upon a 400-acre historic site with century-old oaks, tall pines, winding streams, and colorful dogwoods, the course offers gentle undulations, waste areas and pot bunkers for a Scottish feel. Conditioning has been a problem, particularly in the summer. Still, it's worth a look.

The Heritage Club
Built upon the site of an 18th century rice plantation, the course is sculpted around giant oaks and magnolias, with several holes providing views of the Waccamaw River. Course features undulating fairways and large greens. Large oaks often come into play, requiring accuracy off the tee. Ranked among the top 50 resort courses in America.

Heron Point G.C.
Gently rolling fairways and well-manicured greens. Numerous bunkers and water hazards.

Indian Wells G.C.
Aesthetically pleasing, shotmaker's course with rolling terrain, and plenty of sand and water. Well-bunkered, undulating greens.

Indigo Creek G.C.
Scenic new course with an ample amount of doglegs, bunkers and water. The back nine is set among giant oaks and gently flowing creeks.

Island Green C.C.
Built on gently rolling terrain accentuated by an abundance of azaleas and dogwoods. Several holes feature strategically placed island and peninsula greens, but due to its lack of length, the course isn't overly challenging.

Legends
Ambitious complex featuring three distinct golfing experiences. Heathland is a tribute to the roots of the game, with treeless, wind-swept fairways and deep pot bunkers. Moorland is a fearsome track with deep bunkers, undulating fairways and greens, and signature Dye bulkheads. Parkland, opened in October 1992, offers subtle green contouring, and dramatic, well-placed bunkering. Designed as a tribute to Alister Mackenzie and George Thomas. You have to see this spread to believe it, including the grand St. Andrews-style clubhouse.

Lion's Paw G.L.

New course with dramatic elevations, rolling terrain, expansive fairways, excellent par-threes, and a nice blend of woods and water. A course that requires a great deal of thought, and more than a little skill from the tips with its 74.6 rating.

Litchfield C.C.

One of the area's oldest plantation courses, with mature fairways winding through the site of a former rice plantation. Many giant oaks and large lakes. Also offers an impressive plantation-style clubhouse.

Lockwood G.L.

Excellent course with beautiful river and Intracoastal Waterway views. Tree-lined, non-parallel fairways and water in play on 12 holes. Bentgrass greens are well protected by large sculpted bunkers. Quite a hike from Myrtle Beach (about 60 miles), but worth the trip if you have the time.

The Long Bay Club

The Golden Bear's only public-access course on the Grand Strand, Long Bay was originally private. It's an excellent challenge, with huge sandy waste areas, deep bunkers, elevated greens, and prevailing winds. Ranked in the top 10 in the state by *Golf Digest.* Don't miss it.

Marsh Harbour G.L.

One of the Strand's most heralded courses of the 1980s and still strong enough to be ranked among the top 25 public courses in the U.S. A brilliant collaboration between Dan Maples and developer Larry Young, the course offers elevated ground skirted by low-lying marsh. This allows for naturally elevated tees, fairways and greens, as well as some of the area's best water holes. Watch out for the 570-yard, par-five 17th. This is always a favorite.

Myrtle Beach National

Palmer acted as a consultant on this popular 54-hole complex. North Course features bentgrass greens and an island green par-three. Southcreek Course has been redesigned with bentgrass greens and tight, tree-lined fairways. West Course is more geared to all levels with large greens and cleared forests along the fairways, allowing for easier recovery shots.

Myrtle West G.C.

Pleasant, rolling course offers a variety of challenges with an abundance of sand, water and tall pines. Course is centered around two large canals and also features several small lakes and ponds.

Myrtlewood G.C.

Palmetto Course offers open, rolling coastal terrain, smooth bentgrass greens and a beautiful 18th hole, a 468-yard par-4, that finishes along the Intracoastal Waterway. Pine Hills, designed by Arthur Hills and opened in the spring of 1993, offers gentle elevation changes, numerous water hazards, and bentgrass greens.

Ocean Harbour G.L.

Spectacular setting on a peninsula between the Calabash River and the Intracoastal Waterway. Course offers nine holes along marsh and water. The SC/NC border crosses the course four times, making it possible to play from state to state. Numerous pink and white dogwoods bloom in the spring, adding to the wonderful aesthetics.

Left: Designed as a tribute to legendary designers Alister MacKenzie and George Thomas, Jr., the Parkland Course at the Legends features this strategic par-4, with small yet deep bunkers pinching the landing area around the drive.

Oyster Bay G.L.

Golf Digest's Resort Course of the Year for 1983 and a perennial member of the Best 50 Public Courses in America list. Another Dan Maples, early '80s classic that re-defined golf on the Grand Strand. Winds through tall pines and marshlands, around numerous lakes. Greens are large, well-trapped and undulating. A definitive "must-play" course.

The Pearl G.L.

Both courses are built on a 900-acre marsh preserve, providing for stunning natural beauty. East Course is a traditional layout, carved through a forest and finishing strong along the Calabash River. West is more of a links-style layout with a finish along dramatic bluffs overlooking the Intracoastal Waterway.

Pine Lakes C.C.

The "Granddaddy" of the Strand, where Myrtle Beach golf began. Designer Robert White, the first PGA president and a native of St. Andrews, gave a touch of Scottish flair to the course. Tradition runs rampant here, from the kilted starters to the complimentary cup of Lowcountry clam chowder near the turn. A group of national golf writers convened here for a mini-tournament and outing in 1954; the result was the birth of *Sports Illustrated.* If for nothing else, see it and play it for the tradition.

Possum Trot G.C.

Very playable course with wide fairways and large greens.

Quail Creek G.C.

Wide fairways, and well-placed hazards and bunkers call for a strategic approach.

River Club

Fine plantation course with wide, open fairways and huge, undulating greens. Plenty of water and more than 90 bunkers.

River Hills G. & C.C.

Heavily wooded course with dogwoods, oaks, maples and pines, with frequent elevation changes up to 40 feet. Water comes into play on 13 holes.

Sandpiper Bay G. & C.C.

Rolling, contoured fairways and naturally sculpted bunkers, but the draw here is the greens. They're among the best bentgrass greens on the Grand Strand. A well-maintained course.

Sea Gull G.C.

Wide, non-parallel fairways and large greens with strategically placed bunkers. Course is built on a heavily wooded site of an old plantation. Well-maintained. A Ramada Inn is conveniently located between the 9th and 18th holes.

Surf Club

The third oldest course on the Grand Strand and still one of the best, thanks to a recent rebuilding of all 18 greens. Gently rolling terrain, lush fairways and greens, complemented by colorful azaleas, old oaks and ocean breezes. Definitely worth a visit.

Tidewater G.C. & Plantation

Fabulous new course cited by *Golf* and *Golf Digest* as "Best New Public Course in America" for 1990. Situated on a seaside peninsula of high bluffs, the course offers 10 holes that run along Cherry Grove Inlet or the Intracoastal Waterway. Remaining holes encompass traditional design philosophies, rolling through densely wooded forests and featuring fast (USGA spec), undulating bentgrass greens. A tournament caliber course in every regard, and perhaps the finest course along the Grand Strand. Definitely a "must-play."

Waterway Hills

Early Rees Jones design while still in collaboration with his father, Waterway Hills may be the only course in the world accessible by glass-enclosed gondolas. Three nines offer a variety of hardwoods, lakes and ravines as well as rolling terrain and narrow fairways, some of which roll alongside the Intracoastal Waterway.

Wild Wing Plantation

Ambitious new project developed by Suwaso Corporation of Japan and managed by Western Golf Properties. Wood Stork Course offers a parkland setting with wide fairways enveloped by deep pine forests, and strategically placed water hazards. Hummingbird plays shorter and is more of a links-stly design with gently rolling fairways dotted with pot bunkers and waste areas. Bentgrass greens are small and undulating. The

Avocet Course, opened in early 1993, offers dramatic elevation changes and blends traditional architecture with modern-day design elements. There's a double fairway, a double green, a variety of bunkering, and huge mounds. Work is underway on the fourth course, a Rees Jones design to be called the Falcon Course.

Willbrook Plantation G.C.
Fine plantation course carved from the fertile forests and wetlands of a former Carolina rice plantation. Extensive bunkering, some water.

The Witch
A course as unusual as its name. It winds through wooded hills and wetlands, far from the intrusion of development. The front nine encompasses natural wetland areas, while the back nine offers more rolling terrain. Course also features nearly 4,000 feet of bridges. An interesting, and beautiful, challenge.

Above: The enemies of low scoring in Myrtle Beach are the marshes and the water, and they are often employed extensively, with a chilling effect, on the finishing holes. Pictured here is the final hole on The Pearl's East Course, a tamer of low handicappers from the design studio of Myrtle Beach's most prolific course architect, Dan Maples. Right: The 10th hole at Wild Wing Plantation's Wood Stork Course, designed by Willard Byrd.

The finishing hole at Kiawah Island's Ocean Course, where Bernhard Langer's missed six-footer handed the Ryder Cup trophy back to the Americans in 1991's fabled "War by the Shore".

CHARLESTON

Charleston

The Complete List of Courses Open to the Public

Location	Course	Address
Charleston	Shadowmoss Plantation G.C.	20 Dunvagen Dr.
Edisto Island	*Fairfield Ocean Ridge	Edisto Island
Goose Creek	Crowfield G. & C.C.	300 Hamlet Circle
Hollywood	Links at Stono Ferry	5365 Forest Oaks Dr.
Isle of Palms	Wild Dunes Resort—	
	*Harbor Course	10000 Palmetto Dr.
	**Links Course	10000 Palmetto Dr.
Johns Island	Oak Point G.C.	4255 Bohicket
	Seabrook Island Resort—	
	Crooked Oaks Course	1002 Landfall Way
	Ocean Winds Course	1002 Landfall Way
Kiawah Island	Kiawah Island Resort—	
	Marsh Point	P.O. Box 12357
	**The Ocean Course	P.O. Box 12357
	**Osprey Point	P.O. Box 12357
	**Turtle Point	P.O. Box 12357
Mt. Pleasant	*Charleston National C.C.	Highway 17
	*Dunes West	3535 Wando Plantation Way
	Patriots Point G.C.	P.O. Box 438
N. Charleston	**Coosaw Creek C.C.	4210 Club Course Dr.

* Recommended Course ** Highly Recommended

OVER A SPAN OF SOME 300 YEARS, BEAUTIFUL AND ARISTOCRATIC Charleston has been home to pirates, poets and politicians. It has endured disasters, depressions and economic booms with the same measured dignity. Its unflappable resiliency—no doubt due largely to the strong ties to its own past—has helped make Charleston one of the major port cities on the Eastern Seaboard as well as the cultural capital of the South.

Using history to its best advantage, Charleston has successfully blended its fascinating architecture with innovative planning and development. Its low-profile skyline is punctuated with the spires and steeples of 181 churches, representing 25 denominations, that have sought out Charleston as a haven—it was known for having the most liberal provisions for religious freedom of the 13 original colonies. Later, during the tumultuous years of the Civil War, Charleston served as a center of gentility and culture, of wealthy rice and indigo planters who pleasured themselves with imported luxuries, built magnificent townhouses and held glittering

Rating/Slope: Men	Women	Par	Cost	Phone
70.1/117	70.2/112	72	Moderate	(803) 556-8251
67.8/114	70.3/120	72	n/a	(800) 845-8500
70.5/128	NR	72	Low	(803) 764-4618
68.3/115	68.2/116	72	Low	(803) 763-1817
68.2/117	68.1/117	70	High	(803) 886-6000
69.7/121	69.1/121	72	Very High	(803) 886-6000
69.4/128	69.8/121	72	Moderate	(803) 768-7030
71.2/121	70.1/119	72	Moderate	(803) 768-1000
71.6/125	73.1/127	72	Moderate	(803) 768-1000
69.4/120	67.6/122	71	Very High	(803) 768-2121
74.9/141	72.9/133	72	Very High	(803) 768-2121
68.7/118	69.6/120	72	Very High	(803) 768-2121
71.5/127	71.1/126	72	Very High	(803) 768-2121
71.6/125	70.8/126	72	Moderate	(803) 884-7799
70.7/125	69.2/118	72	Moderate	(803) 856-9378
69.5/113	70.8/115	72	Low	(803) 881-0042
NR	NR	71	Moderate	(803) 767-9000

"socials." Many of those families still own and live in the homes their planter ancestors built, and they still take pride in the beautiful walled gardens, frequently opening them to out-of-town visitors as a gracious welcome to the city.

Indeed, parts of the city appear stopped in time. Block after block of old downtown structures have been preserved and restored for both residential and commercial use. After three centuries of epidemics, earthquakes, fires and hurricanes (including the massive wrath of Hugo in 1988), Charleston has remained one of the South's best preserved cities and one of the last bastions of Old South, antebellum gentility.

But modern-day Charleston is more than just a carefully polished and preserved relic of its past. The city's dedication to the fine arts is evidenced everywhere, from America's oldest museum—The Charleston Museum—to the Dock Street Theatre, the oldest playhouse in the country.

While its historical and cultural allure is well documented, Charleston

The oceanside holes at Kiawah Island's Ocean Course (pictured here, the first and ninth holes) play parallel to the beach, and the resulting off-shore cross-breezes play havoc with shot selection and execution. The result? The Ocean Course's rating, while a playable 72.1 from the white tees, balloons to an astonishing 76.9 (with a slope rating of 149!) from the tips.

has quietly ascended into the forefront as one of the country's great golf destinations as well. Wild Dunes Resort, just north of town on the Isle of Palms, has received worldwide acclaim for its magnificent golf courses and has rebounded strongly from its encounter with Hurricane Hugo. To the south of town is Kiawah Island Resort, one of the South's truly great golf destinations that hosted the 1991 Ryder Cup on its dramatic Pete Dye-designed Ocean Course. In fact, there are probably more oceanfront golf holes per square mile in the Charleston area than anywhere else in the continental U.S. And perhaps you didn't know that the South Carolina Golf Club, the oldest golf club on record in the U.S., was founded in an area in Charleston known as Harleston's Green. The charter was later moved to the Harbour Town Golf Links on Hilton Head Island, and was the inspiration for the creation of the MCI Heritage Classic.

Heritage is a word that fits the city well, from the origins of American golf to the romantic notions of the Old South. While vibrant and progressive, there is no escaping history in Charleston. Ageless and elegant, it is a living museum of America's past.

Getting There

Charleston International Airport is in North Charleston on Interstate 26, about 12 miles west of the city. The airport is served daily by American, Delta and USAir, as well as all major rental car companies. Taxi fare into the city runs about $17; the airport limousine has an $8 fare. Amtrak

The do-or-die finishing hole on Jack Nicklaus' Turtle Point course at Kiawah Island. Sometimes overlooked amidst the controversy and drama surrounding The Ocean Course, Turtle Point has been highly ranked among Carolina courses since it opened in 1981.

arrives at a station in North Charleston, and Greyhound and Trailways both have bus terminals in town. By car, Charleston is accessible via U.S. 17, the main north-south coastal route that passes through town, or via Interstate 26, which runs northwest to southeast and ends in Charleston.

Climate

Charleston's semi-tropical climate, with an average temperature of 65 degrees, makes it suitable for year-round outdoor activity. Warm days and cool nights throughout the winter (average mean highs of 61 degrees, lows of 44 degrees) call for a sweater or light jacket; heavy coats are needed only on rare occasions. Hot summer days and nights (mean highs of 87, lows of 73) are frequently cooled by the breezes off the Atlantic.

Activities

Touring in Charleston is by far the most popular activity, and walking tours are a great (and easy) way to see the city's vast historical treasures. There are two main districts: South of Broad Street, along the waterfront Battery, with an array of historic homes, monuments and parks overlooking the Cooper and Ashley rivers; and North of Broad Street, where you'll find the Old City Market, the Dock Street Theatre, and the Charleston Museum, as well as several old mansions and churches. There are also excellent horse-drawn carriage tours; narrated coach tours that, in season, venture outside of town to the many gardens and plantations; and boat tours that include, among other sites, Fort Sumter—the target of the opening shots of the Civil War—and the aircraft carrier *Yorktown*, which is docked in Charleston Harbor. For sports and recreation, there are several fine beaches in the area for swimming and fishing, and the Charleston Rainbows (the AA farm team of the San Diego Padres) play at College Park Stadium during spring, summer and fall.

Attractions

Charles Towne Landing, a park on the Ashley River and the site of the first permanent English settlement in South Carolina with remains of the original 1670 fortification, beautiful gardens, a replica of a 17th century trading vessel, and a large forest fraught with wildlife; Charleston Museum, America's oldest museum with a fascinating collection of artifacts and treasures that trace the history of the Lowcountry; Magnolia Plantation and Gardens, the country's oldest colonial estate garden with one of the largest collections of camellias and azaleas and featuring the restored plantation house, a 100-acre waterfowl refuge, a three-level observation tower, and a petting zoo for the children; Middleton Place, a

National Historic Landmark and the oldest formal landscaped garden in America with terraced and ornamental grounds, butterfly lakes, and the remains of the original Middleton Place House and Plantation Stableyards; St. Michael's Episcopal Church, the oldest church ediface in the city and one of the few city churches in America to retain its original design, no admission charge; and Thomas Elfe Workshop, a Charleston "single-house" mansion in miniature, built in perfect scale to its larger counterparts prior to 1760 by the city's most famous cabinetmaker.

Shopping

There is excellent shopping in the city; be especially attentive for good buys in antiques and period reproductions, Lowcountry paintings and prints, local craft items, silverware, and designer clothing. King Street is lined with many specialty shops and boutiques; the Old City Market at East Bay and Market streets is a fascinating collection of stalls, specialty shops, and restaurants; The Shops at Charleston Place, on Market Street at the Omni Hotel, is an upscale complex of shops (Gucci, Ralph Lauren, Laura Ashley, Godiva, etc.); and State Street Market, just down from the Old City Market, is another cluster of shops and restaurants.

Popular Dining Options

Barbadoes Room, magnificent Lowcountry specialties and legendary Mud Pie, also features a varied luncheon menu and renowned Sunday brunch, located in the Mills House Hotel; *East Bay Trading Company*, casual, cozy eatery with Continental and American specialties, serving lunch and dinner with a wonderful ambience; *82 Queen*, one of the city's most popular restaurants in a restored 19th century townhouse, serving seafood specialties for lunch and dinner; *Henry's Restaurant*, excellent seafood, beef, fowl and pasta, nightly jazz entertainment; *Le Midi*, popular local spot with superb French country cooking and a great wine list; *Louis's Charleston Grill*, excellent Southern regional cuisine with live jazz nightly, named one of America's best restaurants by *Esquire*; and *Robert's of Charleston*, very small and very elegant with a multi-course, prix-fixe dinner, each course of which is introduced by owner/chef Robert Dickson by song in a rich baritone, don't miss it, but make reservations well in advance.

For More Information

Charleston Trident Convention and Visitors Bureau, P.O. Box 975, Charleston, SC 29402, (803) 577-2510.

THE RESORTS IN DEPTH

Kiawah Island

"Flirting With Perfection, After A Brush With Disaster"

In all fairness, Kiawah Island Resort has had things so well over the past 20 years that something bad was bound to happen. Thanks to an ingenious master plan—headed by the legendary Charles Fraser, he of Sea Pines fame—and an amenity base that rivals any resort property in the world, Kiawah has flirted with perfection virtually since day one. Yet as 1992 came to a close, the resort was righting itself after a brush with disaster that could have proven far more damaging than Hurricane Hugo.

Kiawah Island was thrust into the international spotlight when it hosted the 1991 Ryder Cup, the legendary match where the Americans regained the cup in a nail-biting, white-knuckle finish. Largely responsible for bringing the Ryder Cup to Kiawah Island, as well as the Pete Dye-designed Ocean Course on which it was played, was Landmark Land Company, the Carmel, California-based resort development giant. Landmark Land had purchased the resort's magnificent amenities in 1989 from Kiawah Resort Associates (KRA), a locally owned development company that owned the island's undeveloped land.

When the Landmark Land empire came crashing down in 1992, Kiawah's amenities were included in a package of assets that went up for sale in bankruptcy court. When the court rejected Landmark Land's bid to continue to operate Kiawah in late 1992, the Resolution Trust Company stepped in to operate the resort until a suitable buyer could be found. Meanwhile, KRA continued to own and develop the island's remaining real estate.

Now for the good news: Guests at Kiawah Island during this entire debacle could hardly notice that anything was wrong. The resort was thriving, the flowers were blooming, the golf courses were full, and the overall mood was one of optimism. The Landmark failure was merely an obstacle for a resort that, up until then, had enjoyed the fruits of brilliant planning, prudent development, and successful management.

A 10,400-acre barrier island located 21 miles south of Charleston, Kiawah was first discovered by European settlers in 1688 and was eventually held by the prominent Vanderhorst family for more than 200 years. In 1951, a lumberman from Aiken, S.C., named C.C. Royal bought the island from the Vanderhorst family, built a bridge to the island and

Above left: In addition to his world-famous course at Wild Dunes, Tom Fazio has a hidden gem in the Charleston area: Kiawah Island's Osprey Point course, which was completed in 1986. Pictured here is the 18th hole, which features the excellent mounding for which Fazio is well known for. Above right: A generous bail-out area complements a difficult-to-hit 13th green at Kiawah Island's Ocean Course.

used it as a hunting and fishing retreat for the next 23 years. In 1974, the Kiawah Island Company—a subsidiary of the Kuwait Investment Company—acquired the island for the purpose of creating a residential/resort community. Enter Fraser and his Sea Pines Company, who spent 16 months designing the Kiawah Master Land Use Plan. It is still considered the most thorough land-use plan ever undertaken in America and has won many awards.

Much of Kiawah's resort development took place over the next 14 years including the construction of the Kiawah Island Inn, three 18-hole golf courses, two tennis centers, and various conference and retail areas. But when the Kuwaiti money began to dry up, and the resort was in need of some attention, KRA stepped in and bought the island in June 1988. Landmark came in as the owner and manager of the resort's amenities a year later and built The Ocean Course on a magnificent 2 1/2-mile stretch of oceanfront property at the easternmost tip of the island.

The Ocean Course earned almost instant acclaim as one of Pete Dye's most ambitious (and notorious) works shortly after it opened for play in May 1991. In less than four months—before the worldwide exposure from the Ryder Cup—*Golf* magazine ranked The Ocean Course among its "100 Greatest Courses in the World," making it the youngest course ever to earn the distinction. *Golf Digest*, in turn, named it "America's Best New Resort Course" for 1991.

All 18 holes on The Ocean Course present panoramic views of the Atlantic, and 10 holes play directly along the beachfront. Although the scorecard reads 7,371 yards from the tournament tees, yardage on The Ocean Course is a varied as the ocean wind that constantly sweeps across it. In order to preserve shot value, while accommodating wind conditions and the resort guests that flock to play the course, Dye built several tees on each hole that allow golfers to play the course as short as 4,800 yards.

The Ocean Course complements, without overshadowing, Kiawah's other fine courses. Marsh Point, the resort's first course, is a Gary Player/Ron Kirby collaboration that opened in September 1976. A course of modest length (6,203 yards from the blue tees, 5,841 yards from the whites), Marsh Point features water on 13 holes and has several holes that run along the marsh. The premium here is on accuracy, and there's more than enough trouble awaiting errant shots.

The second of Kiawah's courses, Turtle Point, opened in 1981. This Jack Nicklaus design brought heightened golf attention to the island. It's a championship test—6,919 yards from the tips and 6,396 from the blues— that plays through a maritime forest for 13 holes before exploding with three dramatic oceanfront holes. Ranked as one of the top 75 resort courses in America, Turtle Point has hosted numerous amateur and professional tournaments including the 1990 PGA Cup Matches.

Tom Fazio completed Kiawah's third course, Osprey Point, in 1986. This may be one of the only courses in existence that the owners allowed to mature for two years; it finally opened in September 1988 to rave reviews. Next to The Ocean Course, Osprey Point is the most popular on the island, striking a balance between playability, beauty and challenge (6,678 yards from the blues, 6,015 from the whites). Created among the island's vast marshland and forests and winding around four lakes, Osprey is a dramatic layout that has also been cited among the country's best resort courses.

The resort's other amenities include two separate, full-service tennis facilities with a total of 23 Har-Tru courts and five hard courts; more than 16 miles of paved trails for biking, jogging and walking; a 10-mile, crescent-shaped beach with hobie cat and sailboard rentals on the beach at the Kiawah Island Inn; and some magnificent fishing in the island's ponds, rivers and creeks for spot-tail bass, flounder, sheepshead, croaker and trout, to name a few. Kiawah's recreation program, started in the mid-1970s with a small bike rental operation and a sprinkling of special events, has become one of the country's best, with a wide variety of supervised activities for everyone from three-year-olds to families. Of particular note is "Kiawah Kollege," a participative program for all ages that offers a natural and historical perspective of sea island flora, fauna, wildlife and early plantation living.

Accommodations range from standard guest rooms at the oceanfront

Kiawah Island Inn - located in West Beach Village and within walking distance to several restaurants and lounges, the Straw Market retail shopping complex, West Beach Racquet Club and the Marsh Point clubhouse - or an array of privately owned villas that are spread throughout the resort. All villas are completely furnished and offer fully equipped kitchens, washer/dryer, a living room/dining room area, and from one to four bedrooms. The Kiawah master plan also includes an oceanfront hotel site in the East Beach Village area—adjacent to the Turtle Point golf course and much of the resort's meeting and convention space —as well as a fifth golf course that would be built around the marsh, the 30-acre Bass Pond, and the Kiawah River.

KRA continues to carefully monitor Kiawah Island's development which, regardless of who steps in to take over the resort's amenities, will help to maintain the island's magnificent reputation as a world-class resort destination. That commitment is upheld in the resort's master plan, which continues to serve as the blueprint for the island's future. "From the beginning, Kiawah's development philosophy included a deep devotion to letting nature have its way," reads a company statement on environmental sensitivity, which concludes somewhat ironically: "Man, it was felt, should intrude quietly and with respect."

Hopefully for Kiawah Island, this latest intrusion will depart somewhat more quietly than it arrived.

Seabrook Island
"A Private And Pristine Seaside Resort"

One of my favorite cliches in the resort development business - actually, it's one of those warm and fuzzy marketing pitches - is when a developer claims to be sensitive to the environment by "striking a balance" between man and nature. What this usually means is that they have "struck" down enough trees to build enough condos to help "balance" the budget.

Thankfully, that's never been the case at Seabrook Island, the barrier island resort located 23 miles south of Charleston. There's no such balancing act at Seabrook. Man has never stood a chance at competing with nature here.

Seabrook is so unobtrusively developed that it's hard to believe that anyone really made a go of it here (actually, there have been several owners and managers of the 2,200-acre resort community, but that's another story). Low-rise villas do indeed blend "effortlessly" (another good marketing word) among the surrounding forests, marshlands and

The Crooked Oaks course at Seabrook Island is loaded up with Robert Trent Jones trademarks: Large greens, some severe trapping, and scenic forced carries.

the oceanfront sand dunes. The resort's two golf courses—designed by Robert Trent Jones and Willard Byrd, respectively—meander inland around woods and water hazards and roll out to the ocean. The osprey, alligators, herons, loggerhead turtles and brown pelicans easily outnumber the human inhabitants of the island at any given time. True, Seabrook has never gotten the ink of its famous next-door neighbor, Kiawah Island. Then again, that's sort of been the idea.

The Ryder Cup will probably never be played at Seabrook Island, but that doesn't mean that you shouldn't. The Trent Jones course, Crooked

Oaks, is an inland links-type treatment with tight fairways and elevated greens. This is a very accommodating layout, ranging in length from 5,250 to 6,832 yards, with water coming into play on only about half the holes and less bunkering than is normally found on a Jones course.

Byrd's Ocean Winds course lives up to its name, with five holes (Nos. 10-14) playing alongside the Atlantic. Comparable in yardage to Crooked Oaks, Ocean Winds is more compact with more parallel fairways and much more water. Of particular note are the snaking lagoons that come into play at the fifth (a testy 197 par-3) and sixth holes, as well as the 15th (another good par-3, this one at 180 yards), 16th and 17th.

You'll see more signs of life on the golf courses than you will, say, horseback riding along the 3 1/2 miles of beach or bicycling through a maritime forest or crabbing in one of Seabrook's sheltered creeks. While there's excellent dining on property as well as at the nearby Bohicket Marina, most guests prefer to do it themselves in the privacy of their own villa. For meetings, Seabrook offers complete, state-of-the-art facilities and services to handle groups of up to 300, whose only diversion from the business at hand may be the passing of a shrimping trawler.

So that, in essence, is Seabrook Island—a private, pristine retreat that celebrates the awesome beauty of the Lowcountry barrier islands. No further pitch required...and no developers in sight.

Wild Dunes

"The Revival of a World-Class Golf Retreat"

We're all suckers for a great rise-from-the-ashes success story, and there have been few more impressive in recent years than the one involving Wild Dunes Resort, the 1,600-acre golf and residential retreat located 15 miles north of Charleston.

Wild Dunes rests on the tip of the Isle of Palms, a small barrier island bounded by the Atlantic Ocean, Dewees Inlet and the Intracoastal Waterway. When Hurricane Hugo pounded the Carolina coast in September 1989, the Isle of Palms bore the brunt of much of the storm's fury—winds were unofficially clocked at 187 miles per hour on some areas of the island. The resort at Wild Dunes was obliterated; oceanfront lodging units were reduced to piles of rubble, and the resort's two 18-hole golf courses were covered in debris, sand and salt water.

What followed over the next couple of years was a massive renovation and restoration effort that brought Wild Dunes back from the dead. And from a golf standpoint, the facelift made a great resort even better.

Granted, this was not the first time that long odds had been challenged

The course which put Charleston—and architect Tom Fazio—on the national golfing map was the Links Course at Wild Dunes, which opened in 1980 and was instantly hailed as a masterpiece.

on the Isle of Palms. In Colonial times, while many of the barrier islands were cleared for the planting of sea island cotton, the Isle of Palms was left in its original state—a maze of twisted live oaks and massive sand dunes. The island's northeastern tip—on what is today the 18th hole of the resort's fabled Links Course—was where Lord Cornwallis put ashore his army of Redcoats more than 200 years ago in an attempt to attack Fort Moultrie on neighboring Sullivan's Island. However, the Colonists met and soundly defeated the British, scoring their first major victory of the Revolutionary War.

It was also the site where golf course architect Tom Fazio first fell in love with Wild Dunes. "I saw right away it was an architect's dream," he said in a 1981 interview. "It had all the elements you could ask for - trees, water, dunes, and an ocean coast. The place reminded me of Pine Valley...An architect comes across that kind of land only once or twice in a lifetime."

The result was the Wild Dunes Links Course, described as "a combination of Scotland and the Caribbean" by one national publication, "the ultimate in seaside golf in America" by another, and acclaimed as one of the outstanding courses in the world since its opening on Labor Day 1980. The course was characterized by its rolling, inland front nine with tight fairways flanked by tall pines and ancient oaks, and a back nine that culminated with an oceanside stretch that was unparalleled in its beauty and challenge. Its 18th hole, stretched out against the Atlantic and shaped by the rolling sand dunes, has been called "the greatest finishing hole east of Pebble Beach."

Hugo did its best to blow this grand venue into oblivion, destroying most of the course's wonderful tree cover and leaving the oceanfront par-three 17th and par-five 18th in massive disrepair. Fazio was so distraught after seeing the hurricane's damage to his beloved course that he reportedly refused to return to the site during the massive renovations that followed.

What those renovations did, however, was make Wild Dunes Links a better golf course. All of the greens were rebuilt to USGA specifications and planted in Tifdwarf Bermuda grass, regarded as the best of the Bermuda hybrids and much finer than the 328 strain previously used on the Links Course. Some greens—including that at the 18th—were reshaped slightly to provide for more pin placements. New tees, like those at the par-4 third hole and the par-three 17th, were built to add length to some holes and others, such as the 18th, improved the angle and the definition of the shot that was required. Today, at the 18th, the broad expanse of beach that borders the left side of the hole comes into play off the tee; before Hugo, the massive dunes and limited teeing areas kept the ocean out of play.

These were subtle refinements in many ways, not like those that took place at Wild Dunes' Harbor Course. While the Harbor Course received good reviews upon its opening in 1986, many felt the course was out of balance—there was a easy, short front nine that bordered the Intracoastal Waterway, followed by a long and demanding back nine. Hugo offered the impetus for the resort to completely revamp the Harbor Course, and Fazio supervised the facelift that included the construction of four new holes, significant changes to one existing hole, and a complete rerouting.

The result is a much better mix of long and short holes, a strong par-70 course (the original Harbor Course was a 72) with water and/or marsh on 17 of the 18 holes and more extensive bunkering than on the Links Course. Although the course was shortened to 6,402 yards—nearly 300 shorter than the original—the new routing includes six par-threes, two of which were formerly short par-fours.

Such refinements will obviously go unnoticed to those experiencing Wild Dunes for the first time. It's just another chapter in the life of a still-youthful resort that, after a rough-and-tumble adolescence, continues to achieve greatness beyond its years.

ALSO IN THE AREA

Charleston National C.C.

Beautiful coastal layout that suffered extensive tree damage from Hurricane Hugo, but which has recovered nicely. Surrounded by natural wildlife and marshlands, and practice range overlooks Hamlin Sound.

Coosaw Creek C.C.

New Arthur Hills course that's the centerpiece of a gated residential community in North Charleston, some 20 minutes from downtown. It's a magnificent course, with rolling fairways bounded by marshland and dense forest, and in remarkably good condition despite its youth. A Greenwood Development project (they also developed Palmetto Dunes and Palmetto Hall on Hilton Head Island), Coosaw may well be Charleston's hidden gem and one of its best values.

Crowfield G. & C.C.

Challenging, long course with tree-lined fairways, rolling hills and mounds, and greens protected by bunkers and/or water. Reasonable rates. Food and beverage service on site.

Dunes West
Art Hills course rated one of America's top 10 new resort courses in 1992. Undulating terrain with good finishing holes. Hosted the Amoco-Centel Championship, a PGA-approved event for Tour players over 40. Clubhouse to be completed in 1993.

Fairfield Ocean Ridge Resort
Beautiful layout winding through tropical forest-type surrounding on

Providing excellent facilities, good staffing, and top courses by "name" architects, the growth in "upscale daily fee" courses (like the Arthur Hills-designed Dunes West pictured here) has been one of the most welcome trends in recent years.

small, barrier-island resort. Variety of accommodations available as well as beach and other amenities. Located 40 miles south of Charleston, off Highway 17.

Links at Stono Ferry

Good Ron Garl design that is owned and operated as a public facility by Senior Tour player Jim Colbert. Located 20 minutes from downtown Charleston. Restaurant and lounge on site.

Oak Point G.C.

Scottish-style course packed into a smallish piece of land, thereby limiting the creativity of talented architect Clyde Johnston. Project began as a private club with residential real estate; financial difficulties forced the course to go public.

Patriots Point G.L.

Located directly on Charleston Harbor at the Patriots Point Marine Museum. Lots of lateral water and large greens. Close to the city's historical district.

Shadowmoss Plantation

Pretty course with rolling fairways winding through oak and hickory forests with ponds and streams.

HILTON HE

The justly famed 18th hole at Harbour Town Golf Links, with the Harbour Town Lighthouse in the background.

D ISLAND

Hilton Head Island

The Complete List of Courses Open to the Public

Location	Course	Address
Beaufort	Cat Island G.C.	1 Islands Causeway
	Pleasant Point G.C.	Star Rte. 5, Box 135C
	Golf Professionals Club—	
Bluffton	Champions Course	93 Frances Marion Cir.
	Players Course	93 Frances Marion Cir.
	Executive G.C. (9)	Highway 278
	*Hilton Head National G.C.	Highway 278
	Island West G.C.	Highway 278
	*Old South G.C.	50 Buckingham Plantation
	Rose Hill G.C. (27)	1 Rose Hill Dr.
Callawassie Island	**Callawassie Island (27)	Rte. 1, Box 250
Fripp Island	Ocean Point G.C.	250 Ocean Point Dr.
Hardeeville	Whispering Pines G.C.	Highway 17
Hilton Head Island	*C.C. of Hilton Head	70 Skull Creek Dr.
	*Indigo Run G.C.	72 Colonial Dr.
	Oyster Reef G.C.	155 High Bluff Rd.
	Palmetto Dunes—	
	*Fazio Course	P.O. Box 5859
	**Hills Course	P.O. Box 5859
	*Jones Course	P.O. Box 5859
	Palmetto Hall—	
	Cupp Course	P.O. Box 5859
	**Hills Course	P.O. Box 5859
	Port Royal G.C.—	
	Barony	3 Ben Hook Ct.
	Planter's Row	3 Ben Hook Ct.
	Robber's Row	3 Ben Hook Ct.
	Sea Pines—	
	**Harbour Town G.L.	11 Lighthouse Ln.
	Ocean Course	P.O. Box 5743
	Sea Marsh Course	P.O. Box 5743
	Shipyard G.C. (27)	Shipyard Plantation

* Recommended Course ** Highly Recommended

"I MAY NEVER MAKE ANY MONEY," CHARLES ELBERT FRASER TOLD his mother, "but I want to create something beautiful."

Fraser did indeed create something beautiful. It was Sea Pines Plantation on the remote South Carolina barrier island of Hilton Head, which has become one of the country's most celebrated seaside destinations. And, contrary to the belief of his mother and quite a few pessimistic bankers, Fraser did make some money.

Rating/Slope: Men	Women	Par	Cost	Phone
69.0/122	68.4/116	71	Moderate	(803) 524-0300
69.5/115	69.9/119	71	Moderate	(803) 522-1605
71.2/119	70.8/121	72	Low	(803) 522-9700
66.1/101	68.4/107	72	Low	(803) 522-9700
Executive	Executive	60	Low	(803) 837-6400
69.9/119	66.2/109	72	High	(803) 842-5900
69.9/124	66.5/116	72	High	(803) 757-6660
70.9/125	69.6/123	72	High	(803) 785-5353
71.1/117	70.0/118	72	Moderate	(803) 757-2160
72.4/134	71.0126	72	High	(803) 842-4955
70.1/124	69.6/123	72	High	(803) 838-2309
67.6/113	65.8/102	72	Moderate	(803) 784-2426
71.7/128	71.3/123	72	High	(803) 681-4653
72.2/125	69.3/120	72	Moderate	(803) 689-2200
71.2/123	70.1/119	72	Very High	(803) 681-7717
71.6/126	70.1/117	70	High	(803) 785-1138
69.2/120	67.7/113	72	Very High	(803) 785-1138
69.6/119	70.7/117	72	High	(803) 785-1138
70.1/126	68.6/119	72	High	(803) 689-4100
70.5/123	71.4/119	72	High	(803) 689-4100
69.2/122	70.1/115	72	High	(803) 681-3671
70.6/126	68.9/116	72	High	(803) 681-3671
69.9/124	70.4/114	72	High	(803) 681-3671
68.6/125	68.5/117	71	Very High	(803) 671-2436
71.0/125	69.7/111	72	High	(803) 671-2436
69.6/116	69.8/123	72	High	(803) 671-2436
69.9/123	71.6/119	72	Very High	(803) 785-2402

What mattered more to Fraser, however, was the future of his beloved island. Fraser's father had purchased Hilton Head Island in the 1940s for its prime pine timber, but young Charles had other ideas for Hilton Head's dense coastal forests and marshlands. Rather than let the island fall victim to the "visual pollution" that plagued the East Coast beach resorts of the '40s and '50s, Fraser envisioned stringent, environmentally sound development that blended with the natural surroundings. Sea Pines

Three Hilton Head trademarks: Marshland, water, and an explosion of color. Top left: Callawassie Island's 6th hole on the Dogwood nine, a heroic par-5 reachable in two shots with a perfect drive. Below: The par-3 15th hole at Port Royal's Planter's Row course.

Plantation would ultimately become a model for resort and residential development around the world, and Hilton Head's status as *the* oceanfront destination of choice has reigned supreme for more than 30 years.

At 42 square miles, Hilton Head is the second largest barrier island on the East Coast. It is located at the southeasternmost tip of South Carolina, in the heart of the state's historically and environmentally rich "Lowcountry" area. Those who have traveled to Hilton Head for several years have seen the island change dramatically, yet its allure hasn't faded. The island draws more than 1.5 million visitors annually and boasts a permanent population of around 26,000.

It is an island of great contrasts.

Native islanders coexist with retirees and young professionals. Loggerhead turtles coexist with limousines. There are alligators and attorneys, snowy egrets and shopping malls, and moss-draped oaks and miniature golf. There are those who condemn the island's "blatant" commercialism, and while Hilton Head certainly has had an influx of fast-food haunts, economy motels, and outlet shopping centers, the island remains only about 40 percent developed.

What you can't take away from Hilton Head are its abundant assets. In addition to its astounding natural beauty, there are 12 miles of magnificent beaches with some of the finest resort hotels on the Atlantic coast; more than 300 tennis courts of all three Grand Slam surfaces - clay, hard and grass; and, perhaps best of all, more than 20 fine golf courses. The surrounding Lowcountry area— ranging south to the Georgia border near the scenic port city of Savannah and north to the historical town of Beaufort—offers nearly a dozen more golf courses. Hilton Head is also becoming renowned for its thriving arts environment: its Community

Playhouse and orchestra are remarkable for a town of this size, and plans are underway on a multi-million-dollar Cultural Center.

Having founded its modern roots as a vacation resort, Hilton Head Island has blossomed into a bona fide community, one which mirrors the standards of excellence upon which this grand resort was built. Charles Fraser did, in fact, create something beautiful here. And to his eternal credit, it's a beauty that is timeless.

Getting There

The Hilton Head Airport is served daily by USAir Express from Charlotte, N.C., and American Eagle from Raleigh-Durham, N.C. There are a limited number of flights from Atlanta on GP Express, a privately-owned commuter service. Savannah International Airport is 50 minutes from

Hilton Head and is serviced by Delta, American, United, and USAir. Rental cars, limousines and shuttle services are available from both Hilton Head and Savannah airports, and taxi service is also available.

Weather

Hilton Head Island's climate is generally characterized as "semi-tropical." The summers, which run from mid-May to September, tend to be hot and humid with frequent afternoon thunderstorms. Winter temperatures range from the 60s during the day into the 40s at night. The spring and fall are, in a word, perfect: Warm days (mid-70s) and cool nights (mid-50s).

Activities

For golfers and non-golfers alike, there's the beach and all its inherent

Left: A Scottish-style double green joins the 9th and 18th holes at popular Hilton Head National. Opened in 1990 from a Gary Player design, its relatively short length has made it a special favorite of women golfers. Below: The daunting oceanside par-5 10th hole at the Robert Trent Jones course in Palmetto Dunes.

amenities: the typical (swimming, boardsailing, sailboat rentals) and the unusual (jet-skiing, hydro-sled tubing, parasailing). There are also guided beach walks that focus on the area's rich ecosystems and their preservation. Horseback riding through the 605-acre Sea Pines Forest Preserve offers a glimpse of what Hilton Head was like before Charles Fraser and Sea Pines. So do the many historical tours conducted by the Museum of Hilton Head, which explore relics of the island's past, from antebellum ruins to Civil War remnants. For a real taste of the Lowcountry, try crabbing in the local waters with a string, a chicken neck and a large net. If you're patient enough, you'll end up with a real feast.

Attractions

Hilton Head's most recognizable landmark is Harbour Town, with its familiar red-and-white-striped lighthouse and circular marina surrounded by a quaint village of shops and restaurants. Gregg Russell's nightly singing performances under the Liberty Oak (in season) are a must for visitors with children. Adventure Cruises, based out of Shelter Cove Marina, offers a variety of adventures including Daufuskie Island tours, dolphin encounters, murder mystery cruises, sunset dinner cruises and deep-sea fishing trips. For the arts, the best continually running show in town is the Hilton Head Playhouse, with top-notch year-round productions. The annual Christmas production is an island tradition, often featuring local celebrities like author John Jakes.

Shopping

The island's only enclosed complex is the Mall at Shelter Cove, with more than 55 shops—including Polo, Banana Republic and Victoria's Secret—and restaurants. There's been a recent infusion of "factory-direct" outlet centers in and around Hilton Head including Shoppes on the Parkway, Pineland Mill Shops and Lowcountry Factory Village. The island's oldest shopping center is Coligny Plaza, an oceanside complex with more than 50 shops, a theatre, and several good restaurants. Some of the island's more upscale shopping areas include the marina villages of Harbour Town and Shelter Cove, and Sea Pines Center, located inside Sea Pines Plantation with some fine clothing, jewelry and craft shops, a large grocery store, and a wonderful restaurant, Truffles.

For More Information

Hilton Head Island Chamber of Commerce, P.O. Drawer 5647, Hilton Head Island, SC 29938, (803) 785-3673.

Popular Dining Options

Cherrystone's, outstanding fresh seafood as well as pasta, beef and veal dishes and a terrific wine list, owned by local culinary legend Fulvio Valsecchi; *Old Oyster Factory*, magnificent water views of Broad Creek and a nice range of fresh fish, shellfish and other items; *Crazy Crab*, a vibrant, popular spot with two locations—North Island and Harbour Town, excellent stuffed flounder and hush puppies to die for; *Scott's*, moderately priced fare ranging from seafood to steaks in a great waterfront setting in Shelter Cove; *Alexander's*, a local landmark in Palmetto Dunes with great food and attentive service in a casual atmosphere, don't miss the duckling; *The Chart House*, casual steak-and-seafood eatery on the docks at Palmetto Bay Marina, serves perhaps the finest prime rib on the island; *The Quarterdeck*, a longtime favorite saloon that now serves lunch and dinner, the sunsets are extraordinary; *Truffles*, a popular lunch spot with locals in Sea Pines Center, excellent French bread sandwiches, baked brie, and a heavenly curried chicken salad; *Cafe Europa*, fresh seafood and European specialties in a waterfront setting at the Harbour Town lighthouse; *Fitzgerald's*, an island favorite for nearly 20 years, an elegant room that specializes in beef, veal and seafood dishes; *Harbourmaster*, sophisticated setting with outstanding cuisine and impeccable service, located on the water at Shelter Cove, jackets required; *Juleps*, a gracious, Southern-flavored room operated by longtime islander Ed Murray, elegant but personable with fare ranging from seafood to beef, veal, pasta and homemade desserts; *The Gaslight*, a Mobil Three-Star restaurant with classic French cuisine in an elegant candlelit setting; *La Maisonette*, also rated Three Stars but somewhat touristy, with a prix fixe menu in a relaxed, intimate atmosphere; *Cafe at Wexford*, country French cuisine and setting, popular lunch haunt for locals; *Charlie's L'Etoile Verte*, an obscure, tiny French cafe near Palmetto Dunes with wonderful food—the limited menu is written on a mirror hanging over the kitchen.—the home of the Hilton Head power lunch; *Antonio's*, Southern Italian cuisine located in the Village at Wexford; *The Little Venice*, Northern Italian cuisine on the water at Shelter Cove; *Primo*, creative, contemporary Italian dishes in one of the island's most attractive settings; *San Miguel's*, long-time island favorite with great combination platters and margueritas, waterfront setting at Shelter Cove Marina with outdoor seating; *Kyoto Japanese Steak and Seafood House*, samurai chefs perform tableside, dinner only.

THE RESORTS IN DEPTH

Sea Pines
"Where It All Began"

There should always be a prelude to any narrative regarding Sea Pines, Hilton Head Island's renowned resort and residential community. Devoting a thousand or so words to the Sea Pines story is like reading the Cliff Notes version of *War and Peace,* or writing a thumbnail sketch of the Renaissance. Truth is, the tale of this storied 4,500-acre community offers all the elements of a classic piece of literature: history, intrigue, success, failure, tragedy, and drama. Sounds like a great novel. For these purposes, however, you'll have to settle for the slightly condensed version.

Lauded worldwide for its master planning and the extraordinary vision of its creator, Charles Fraser, Sea Pines has been to the heights of success and the depths of despair. After a shaky decade in the '80s that included several ownership changes, mis-management, and a turbulent 18-month stint in Chapter 11 bankruptcy, Sea Pines has reemerged in the '90s as one of the South's most prominent seaside destinations.

Sea Pines was one of the first, and is still one of the best, self-contained resort destinations in the U.S. Its range of recreational amenities remains unparalleled: Three public-access golf courses including the Harbour Town Golf Links, perennially ranked among the top 75 golf courses in the world; the 30-court Sea Pines Racquet Club, which has hosted the prestigious Family Circle Cup women's professional tournament for the past 20 years; a five-mile stretch of beach that ranks among the most scenic on Hilton Head; two marinas with adjacent shopping villages; miles of bicycle paths; a stable that has hosted several top equestrian events; more than 500 rental homes and condominiums and a variety of restaurants offering everything from snacks to Continental cuisine.

Still, the Sea Pines story is not so much what is there, but how it was put there. Guided by Fraser's ingenious and unprecedented land-use planning, Sea Pines set the standard for which countless other resort communities have followed (most notably, neighboring Kiawah Island and Amelia Island Plantation, both of which originally were Sea Pines Company properties). Today, as it was 35 years ago, Sea Pines is a unique community dually blessed by the engineered handiwork of man and the uncontrived artfulness of Mother Nature.

Fraser's first visions for the development of Sea Pines Plantation began in 1950. As a 21-year-old University of Georgia graduate, Fraser spent the

Harbour Town's collection of par-3 holes are routinely rated among the best in the world, including the do-or-Dye 14th.

summer working on Hilton Head with his father's timbering company before entering Yale Law School that fall. While exploring the south end of the island on a logging tractor, Fraser believed that something very special could be done with the primitive, yet breathtakingly beautiful piece of land. It wouldn't be the Coney Island-ish type of development that typified the beach resorts of the 1940s—that thought horrified Fraser. Rather, his community would enhance the natural environment with strict architectural and land-use guidelines while offering a full array of recreational amenities. Not only could the land be successfully developed, thought Fraser. It could be successfully preserved as well.

Charleston bankers and other potential financiers of Fraser's proposed venture weren't nearly as impressed. Seeing Hilton Head Island as "devoid of modern civilization," lenders advised Fraser that no prominent families were building beach homes anymore. and that all seasonal summer homes were being built only in the mountains. Furthermore, South Carolina was an extremely poor state and one that offered virtually nothing to the upscale vacationer from the Northeast and Midwest. Hilton Head, they advised, for useful only for growing pine trees.

Nevertheless, Fraser set off with a 90-page economic impact study, and a considerable amount of blind faith, and incorporated the Sea Pines Plantation Company in 1957. And in time, several South Carolina textile and insurance executives took an interest in Fraser's fresh approach to community planning and not only purchased property at Sea Pines, but encouraged other affluent friends to do so as well. But Fraser didn't make it easy. It wasn't enough that he was luring these well-to-do people to this mosquito and alligator-plagued island. He would also attach some 40 pages of ironclad restrictions to every deed (a "reverse bill of rights," suggested one wag at the time). The No. 1 restriction: Fraser could disallow any housing plan for any reason. Take it or leave it.

Although Fraser did have to buy a few lots back, most of the early

The perilous par-3 15th hole at the Ocean Course in Sea Pines is one of only two oceanfront holes on Hilton Head Island (the other is the 10th hole at the Robert Trent Jones Course in Palmetto Dunes). Typically playing directly into the wind, this par-3 rarely yields a birdie.

settlers decided to stick it out. Good move. By 1962, Sea Pines had been lauded by scores of national publications and honored by a variety of architectural and environmental organizations. Oceanfront lots that had sold for just over $9,000 in 1960 jumped to $20,000 four years later. Those lots today? A half-million-dollars, on up.

In 1966, Sea Pines opened its second golf course, Sea Marsh (the first, Ocean, debuted in 1960). During an opening exhibition match, a young Jack Nicklaus urged Fraser to let him and a still relatively unknown architect named Pete Dye design the plantation's third course. Fraser complied, and in November 1969 the Harbour Town Golf Links opened just in time to host a PGA tournament, the Sea Pines Heritage Classic. The Harbour Town course garnered immediate widespread attention, thanks in part to Arnold Palmer winning the inaugural Heritage Classic and the subsequent opening of the Harbour Town marina and its familiar red-and-white-striped lighthouse, which has since become a worldwide symbol for both Sea Pines and Hilton Head Island.

Just as he had succeeded with his masterful planning of Sea Pines as a residential community, Fraser's vision was sharp when it came to Sea Pines' major recreational drawing card: golf. The Ocean, Sea Marsh, and Harbour Town courses are all distinctively different and offer varying degrees of difficulty to resort guests. The Sea Pines Club Course, designed by Palmer and opened in 1974, is a members-only layout.

Sea Marsh, designed by the late George Cobb, features broad, tree-lined fairways that traverse several large lagoons and marshes. Playing to a manageable 6,169 yards from the regular tees (6,515 from the tips), Sea Marsh offers its most tempting challenge at the 471-yard, par-5 ninth hole, a sharp dogleg left where the second shot must be played over water to an elevated green enveloped by bunkers and backed by marshland.

The Ocean Course is also a Cobb design that features one of the most photographed holes on Hilton Head, the dastardly 207-yard par-three 15th. The tee shot at 15 is played straight out to the ocean, most times directly into the teeth of the wind. The narrow green slopes severely uphill and is surrounded by four large bunkers. Despite the presence of several shorter, more forgiving holes (the course plays from 5,284 to 6,614 yards), the finishing stretch, beginning at 15, is one of the most challenging on the island.

Then there's the Harbour Town Links, which will forever serve as a monument to Southern coastal golf courses. Harbour Town is unquestionably one of the great lowland courses in the U.S., with 6,900 yards of tight, twisting fairways flanked by grand oaks and towering pines. Because Dye built the course so low to the ground, there are many opportunities to pitch and run the ball onto the greens. That's good, because the greens at Harbour Town are about as large as the average regulation-sized pool table. Because the Bermuda greens are overseeded every fall with Bentgrass, they tend to putt that way, too.

Although every hole at Harbour Town has its own unique character, the back nine presents one formidable challenge after another. There's the 378-yard 13th, a tight little test that ranks as one of the best short par-fours in the country. The hole plays to a green raised out of a horseshoe-shaped bunker by cypress planks. Alice Dye, Pete's wife, takes credit for creating the green at 13 and has noted that certain players have found it easier to putt up the side of the planks rather than trying to hold a sand shot on the flat, narrow putting surface.

The 165-yard, par-three 14th hole is one of the prettiest on the golf course—all carry over water with overhanging oaks to the left and a nasty pot bunker to the rear. Beauty is in the eyes of the beholder, however. Ask Tom Watson, a two-time Heritage Classic winner who snatched defeat from the jaws of victory several years ago by dropping one into the drink on Sunday, or Ben Crenshaw, who hit four straight balls into the water one year en route to a smooth 12.

The par-five 15th at Harbour Town has garnered significant praise from touring pros through the years. At 575 yards, 15 will yield its fair share of pars, but birdie is another story. For starters, you can pretty much forget about getting home in two. The hole turns subtly to the left, with the green tucked behind a small lagoon and flanked by bunkers. The smart play is a long-iron second shot out to the right of the fairway, and a wedge into the two-tiered green. This green, once a postage stamp, has been enlarged in recent years. But unlike the old days, where you felt you had a decent chance from anywhere on the tiny green, an accurate approach is now vital to preventing three putts.

The severity of Harbour Town's finishing hole, a 478-yard par-four, depends almost exclusively on the wind. Winding along the marshes of Calibogue Sound, the hole can play extremely difficult in a crossing wind or a headwind; in fact, sometimes it's virtually impossible to get home in two. But when there's a tailwind, or no wind at all, the hole can play fairly tame. When Payne Stewart won his second consecutive MCI Heritage Classic title in 1991, he played the hole on Sunday with a driver and an eight-iron in calm conditions. Still, there are few tournament venues whose finishing hole can compete with Harbour Town for drama and memorability, with the familiar lighthouse looming in the background. The hole has certainly provided its share of drama over the past several years. You probably recall the 1988 MCI Heritage Classic, when Greg Norman saved par at 18 with a clutch three-foot putt to preserve his first win at Harbour Town, which he promptly dedicated to leukemia victim Jamie Hutton.

It may all sound a little like a fairy tale, and there are many who remember some of the dark days of Sea Pines - but those days are long gone. Sea Pines has re-established itself as a prime resort destination as well as a successful, thriving residential community. And everyone, it seems, is living happily ever after.

Palmetto Dunes
"Thriving on the Conservative Approach"

Like many resort areas in the Sun Belt, Hilton Head Island has taken its image lumps over the past few years. The S&L debacle, the recession and tax reforms in 1986 spelled doom to some developers and certainly Hilton Head wasn't exempt from the tumult. But one Hilton Head developer,

Above right: One of the most demanding courses on the Island, the Fazio course at Palmetto Dunes combines length and extensive trapping into an enthralling and testing golf experience. Pictured here is the par-4 16th. Below right: The 18th at the Arthur Hills Course at Palmetto Hall is one of the most respected anywhere; the approach flirts with water all the along the left side.

Greenwood Development Corporation not only weathered the storm but earned a solid fiscal reputation in the process.

Sure, everyone at Greenwood would like to think that it's because they're so smart. And while they are pretty sharp folks, it's primarily because the company is a subsidiary of Greenwood Mills, a family-owned textile company that's been around for more than 100 years. It is a financially sound and fiscally conservative operation.

Having a strong parent company becomes extremely beneficial in the lean times. Greenwood Development was very busy during the worst of times on Hilton Head, developing oceanfront property in its flagship resort, Palmetto Dunes; developing the island's only shopping mall and a nearby deep-water marina known as Shelter Cove; and more recently, developing Palmetto Hall, a new residential golf community on the island's north end.

Greenwood has never tried a lot of gimmicks to be successful; such measures were never needed. The 2,000-acre Palmetto Dunes has proven to be a model of consistency over the years, successfully serving as a growing residential community and a thriving, active resort with two major oceanfront hotels, three outstanding golf courses, and an overall amenity base that, with the possible exception of neighboring Sea Pines , is unparalleled for both quality and quantity.

Designed respectively by Robert Trent Jones, George Fazio and Arthur Hills, the golf courses in Palmetto Dunes offer distinctively different design elements. Even the topography is different, although the courses are a short distance from one another within the resort.

The oldest of the trio, the Jones Course, is probably the most user-friendly and among the most picturesque layouts on Hilton Head Island. Winding through parts of an 11-mile network of navigable lagoons, the Jones Course is also among the most visible on the island, since four of its holes run parallel with the island's main thoroughfare, William Hilton Parkway (Hwy 278). The 10th hole is the course's signature, a par-five playing 540 yards from the blue tees straightaway to a green set hard against the Atlantic beachfront. The course measures 6,710 yards, with a slope rating of 123.

The Fazio Course is not for those whose games still have training wheels. Measuring 6,873 from the tips, its has only two par-fives and plays to a par of 70. From the gold tees, the course rating is 74.2, the highest in the Hilton Head area, and the slope is 132. Even from the white tees, (6,239 yards), the course rating is 71.2 and the slope, 123. The two buzz words here are "long" and "sand." While the course boasts only 57 bunkers, some of the fairway traps seem to go on for days. The terrain is more rolling here than the relatively flat Jones Course, which makes these long par-fours play that much longer.

The newest of the three courses, the Hills Course, has entirely different character than the Jones or Fazio courses. Built in part on an old secondary sand dune line, the Hills Course features dramatically rolling fairways which flow into the greens. The course has hosted the Palmetto Dunes/*Golf World* Collegiate since 1986 and was the site of the NCAA Women's Championship in 1990.

Measuring a modest 6,651 yards from the blue tees, the Hills Course is a par-72 that's rated 71.2/127. But those figures are somewhat misleading, since water comes into play on 10 holes and ocean breezes can quickly turn the course into a beast. PGA touring pro Robert Gamez, for example, set the Hills course record in 1988 while playing in the Collegiate. He opened with a 65, shot 75 in the wind on the second day, and closed with a 64.

The 17th hole, just 380 yards from the tips, illustrates how fickle the Hills Course can be: fairly benign on a calm day and downright scary with the wind blowing. It is a sharp dogleg left, almost horseshoe-shaped, with water running down the left side off the tee and crossing over in front of a very shallow green on the approach.

Though resort golf is a very large egg in its product basket, Palmetto Dunes revels in many other amenities. The Palmetto Dunes Tennis Center, formerly known as the Rod Laver Tennis Center, is consistently ranked among the top resort facilities in the nation. Tennis exhibitions are conducted every Monday night throughout the summer. There's also three miles of Atlantic beaches to comb.

On the inland side of the resort, Shelter Cove boasts the largest, deepest marina on the island. The 15.5-acre marina contains 170 slips and can accommodate boats of up to 120 feet. For the angler, Shelter Cove annually hosts two fishing tournaments, one for king mackerel and cobia in June and again for kings in August.

The Shelter Cove Marina is also the site of Harbourfest, which has become one of the island's biggest summertime draws for visitors and residents alike. A festival of music, food, arts and crafts, and fireworks, Harbourfest is sponsored by Greenwood Development and runs every Tuesday from 6 to 9:30 p.m. from June 2 through Labor Day. The 240-acre marina village also has a variety of shops, restaurants and waterfront villas.

Palmetto Dunes also offers virtually every conceivable accommodation, including more than 500 rental homes and villas in all sizes and settings, and two excellent oceanfront hotels, the 505-room Hyatt Regency Hilton Head and the 325-room Hilton Resort. The Hyatt, regarded as one of the Southeast's major meeting and convention destinations, is also known island-wide for its fine dining and its energized bottom-floor nightclub, Club Indigo. The Hilton, formerly known as Mariner's Inn, is more laid back, set amid lush gardens and fountains that lead out to the beach and featuring oversized guest rooms and suites with fully equipped mini-kitchens.

While Greenwood sees build-out of its Hilton Head properties within the next decade, the company isn't planning to go anywhere. It will remain in an operations mode indefinitely, which will ultimately give Palmetto Dunes a rather exemplary distinction. It will be Hilton Head Island's most successful, and longest-lasting community under one owner/operator.

So you can call Greenwood Development conservative, or perhaps even old-fashioned, in its business principles. But you can also call it successful, and as one old-timer once put it, you can take that to the bank.

Shipyard Plantation
"Quintessential Hilton Head"

Shipyard Plantation may be the most active, vibrant resort community on Hilton Head Island, thus making it a popular destination for island visitors Encompassing only 837 acres in the south-central portion of the island, Shipyard offers a fine oceanfront resort hotel, a golf club that has hosted a Senior PGA Tour event, and an outstanding racquet club where several major tournaments have been played.

If you choose to rent a villa for your Hilton Head vacation, there's a good chance you'll end up in Shipyard. You shouldn't be disappointed. There are well over 700 villas and condominiums in Shipyard, many of which have been around for awhile but have been well maintained. Like many of the island's plantations, the natural aesthetics have been meticulously maintained in Shipyard, and many villa complexes blend effortlessly with the surrounding moss-covered oaks and other native vegetation. Many villas are sited along Shipyard's 27 holes of golf, which enhances the atmosphere.

Shipyard Golf Club, originally known as the Hilton Head Golf Club, is one of the oldest on the island. Willard Byrd teamed with the late George

The second hole on Shipyard's Brigantine nine is Alligator Capital of Hilton Head during the spring mating season, and a gallery of up to twenty amorous saurians may be on hand as you negotiate the approach shot on this daunting par-4.

Cobb on the design of the original 18 holes, which encompass the Galleon and Clipper nines. This is quintessential Hilton Head Island resort golf: tight, narrow fairways enveloped by towering pines, magnolias and oaks, with an abundance of sand and water. The greens are typically large with significant undulation. Playing to 6,830 from the tips, the Galleon/Clipper rota is among the most popular courses on Hilton Head for resort guests. It was also strong enough to host the PGA Seniors International for three years in the mid-1980s. The newer nine, Brigantine, is also a Byrd design. This is also a tight testing course where the driver is best left in the bag, and the water hazards are much more pronounced.

The other signature amenity in Shipyard is the 20-court Shipyard Racquet Club, inarguably the most beautiful setting for a tennis facility on the island with courts dotted through a proverbial forest of native flora and fauna. Billie Jean King, an early Shipyard property owner, had a hand in the design of the club, which has been the site of several professional tournaments. A gangly, unknown 14-year-old German named Steffi Graf made her first Hilton Head appearance here during the World Couples Invitational mixed doubles event in the mid-1980s; she would, a few years later, win her first professional title at the nearby Sea Pines Racquet Club during the Family Circle Magazine Cup. Today, Shipyard Racquet Club serves as a major instructional facility for international-known teacher Dennis Van der Meer.

Adjacent to the racquet club, on a marvelous stretch of beach, is the new Crystal Sands Resort, an upscale Holiday Inn-managed Crowne Plaza hotel that for years was Marriott's Hilton Head Resort. The 338-room hotel was totally renovated during the winter of 1992-93 and offers an array of fine amenities including indoor and outdoor pools, two restaurants, a popular lounge, a health and fitness club, and expansive meeting and banquet facilities, all in a beautiful garden-oriented setting. The Crystal Sands was Holiday Inn's first Crowne Plaza resort in the continental U.S.

Whether you're a guest of the hotel or renting a private villa, perhaps the best way to get around Shipyard is by its network of bike paths that run throughout the plantation. It's certainly the best way to experience the plantation's astounding beauty. Despite the extensive resort and residential development that has taken place in Shipyard, the aesthetics have been remarkably maintained. In that regard, the plantation is a fitting testament to the Hilton Head ideal, and a very popular one at that.

Rees Jones has designed four Hilton Head area courses. The elegant Country Club of Hilton Head, pictured here at the par-5 8th hole, is one of two open to the public.

The Westin Resort
"Oceanfront Luxury That Flirts With Perfection"

Most travelers would be taxed to pinpoint exactly what it is that separates an outstanding hotel from an unparalleled one. Those inside the industry know better. Westin certainly knows better. The Seattle-based hotel/resort management company realizes that, in the hospitality industry, greatness is measured by one simple overriding factor. It is service, with a capital "S." If it's a property that's based in the South, the self-proclaimed capital of gracious hospitality, the expectations become somewhat greater.

Thus, Westin obviously takes great pride in its 410-room resort hotel at Hilton Head Island in Port Royal Plantation. Long the jewel of the island's hotel properties - starting in 1985 when it was built, owned and managed by the posh Inter-Continental chain - the Westin Resort on Hilton Head is one of a handful of Southern properties to boast the AAA Five-Diamond designation. Having held Mobil's Four-Star status every year since its opening, the resort is flirting with perfection these days. As guests of the Westin will testify, a "Perfect 10" is certainly within reach.

On the surface, it appears that Hilton Head's Westin Resort lacks little of what it takes to be a Five Star/Five Diamond property. Situated on a 24-acre oceanfront tract in Port Royal Plantation, the hotel was built by Inter-Continental in 1985 at a cost of $70 million. While its green spires, green gabled roof and white pillar columns are reminiscent of turn-of-the-century grand seaside resort hotels, the exterior design also emits a Charlestonesque flavor in celebration of the rich heritage of its setting in the Carolina Lowcountry.

The interior of the hotel further reflects the traditional Southern influence with wood-planked floors, period antiques and Oriental rugs. Yet the elegance is relaxed and understated, not intimidating. In other words, you know you're in a fine hotel, but you shouldn't be afraid to sit on the furniture.

Guest rooms at the Westin, almost all of which feature expansive ocean views, incorporate liberal use of glass, brass and pine with king-sized beds, separate sitting areas with loveseat and lounge chair, pine armoirs, and large baths with built-in hairdryers and telephones. The hotel's 38 suites each resemble a small residence with separate living and dining rooms, and some include grand pianos, Jacuzzis, saunas and steam baths.

As with most major resort hotels, the Westin's group and convention business easily outdistances its social, tourist-oriented traffic. Although not surprising - the hotel offers award-winning conference facilities with more than 25,000 square feet of meeting and banquet space catering to groups from 10 to 2,000—the resort offers enough activities and services to keep the average family busy for the better part of the summer. In fact, perhaps the best thing about staying at the Westin is that one can be as active, or as lazy, as one desires.

The hotel offers access to 36 holes of the 54 holes of golf at Port Royal Plantation. Two of the Port Royal courses—Barony and Robber's Row—alternate as private for member play only from month to month, while the third course, Planter's Row, is open for guest play year-round.

Barony and Robber's Row are both products of the late Augusta-based designer, George Cobb. Barony, which plays to 6,530 yards and par 72 from the championship tees, presents its greatest challenge around the small greens, heavily protected by deep bunkers, lagoons and Bermuda rough. Robber's Row, which plays slightly longer at 6,711 yards, features tight fairways lined with oaks and magnolias and winds through marshy land that once served as the site of the Civil War town of Port Royal. In fact, one of the truly unique aspects of the golf courses at Port Royal is that golfers get a miniature history lesson on every hole. The tee boxes feature markers that describe significant landmarks or events that took place on the site during the war years. At this writing, Pete Dye is overseeing a major renovation of the Robber's Row course.

Port Royal's newest course, Planter's Row, opened in 1983 and served as host site for the PGA Seniors International tournament in 1985. The Willard Byrd design, measuring 6,520 yards from the tips, reflects the architect's philosophy that golf is a game of accuracy. Tree-lined parallel fairways are dotted with treacherous bunkers and water hazards, and the large greens are severely undulating.

Westin Resort guests are also afforded use of the Port Royal Racquet Club, one of only a handful of tennis facilities in the U.S. to offer all three Grand Slam surfaces with 10 Har-Tru (clay) courts, four Deco (hard) courts, and two grass courts. The facility has been an annual Five-Star recipient from tennis industry publications and offers a variety of private and group lessons and clinics. If you're visiting in the summer, you'll probably catch a glimpse of Martina Navratilova, who frequently works out on the grass and hard courts at Port Royal in preparation for Wimbledon and the U.S. Open.

On-site amenities at the Westin Resort include a fully-equipped health club and spa with Universal Paramount equipment, free weights, fitness testing, a full-time massage therapist and complimentary daily exercise classes for hotel guests. There are three swimming pools, ranging from a 4,800-square-foot outdoor lap pool to a 840-square-foot indoor facility; three outdoor whirlpools; and a children's program, Kid's Korner, that offers a full range of activities for ages 5-12 as well as teens.

As for dining and entertainment, the Westin offers perhaps the finest array of restaurants and lounges on Hilton Head Island. Continental and Lowcountry fare is served in an elegant Country French setting at The Barony, while more casual all-day dining—as well as a spectacular Sunday brunch—is served in the Carolina Cafe. The Playful Pelican offers cocktails and entertainment in an oceanfront setting, while Pelican Poolside serves light lunches and snacks poolside. Each afternoon in The Gazebo, a comfortable sitting-room lounge just off the main lobby, tea and hors d'oeuvres are served by a crackling fire during the winter months, with cocktails and light jazz offered throughout the seasonal periods.

But awe-inspiring physical plants and a vast array of amenities do not alone win the hearts of the folks who conduct the Mobil ratings. In its continued commitment to guest service, the hotel offers 24-hour, seven-day room service; same-day valet service from its in-house laundry; twice-daily maid service with nightly turn-down; valet parking; and 24-hour, seven-day on-site management, providing guests with an around-the-clock liaison with management.

So there's no magic formula in making the entire program work. It simply takes a great deal of time and effort, from the training of the management to the recruitment of the employees. It's a commitment to the highest possible level of service, and the Westin Resort on Hilton Head has it down to—almost—perfection.

ALSO IN THE AREA

Arthur Hills Course, Palmetto Hall Plantation

Terrific new layout named as one of country's ten best new resort courses in 1991. Quintessential Art Hills design; gently rolling and weaving in and out of dense forests of oak, pine and willow trees and natural wetlands. Part of a 750-acre residential community developed by Greenwood Development Corporation, parent company of Palmetto Dunes Resort.

Callawassie Island Club

Outstanding Fazio design that has never achieved the notoriety it deserves. Unusually high elevation for the Lowcountry area allowed for extreme undulations, and there's plenty of mounds, swales and dramatic bunkering. The newest nine, Dogwood, is equally as scenic as Palmetto and Magnolia—its final four holes play alongside the marshes of

Chechessee Creek—but it lacks the character of the original 18. Still, this is well worth the 30-minute trip from Hilton Head Island or Beaufort.

Cat Island Club
Scenic design that plays inland through a densely wooded forest and out to serene coastal marshlands. As with many Cobb designs, numerous doglegs call for strict placement off the tee. Particularly unique and demanding are the par-3s, including back-to-back one-shotters at No. 4 and 5 that require full carries over beautiful expanses of marsh. The course is located on a 432-acre barrier island, two miles southeast of Beaufort and 35 minutes from Hilton Head.

Country Club of Hilton Head
Rolling course that rambles through wide open expanses, pine and oak woodlands, freshwater ponds and marshes. Heavily contoured fairways and undulating greens, pot and sculpted bunkers, and grass hollows give this course a great deal of character, and make it a superb test. The Country Club of Hilton Head was recently honored in *Links Magazine* as an excellent example of playability in course design.

The Executive G.C.
Lighted executive course that's enjoyable for families and beginners. Undulating greens offer two pin placements to suit a variety of skill levels. Tight fairways, strategic water hazards, and an island green.

The Golf Professionals Club
Champions Course winds through tall stands of pines and is one of the area's longest courses. Players Course winds through forests of moss-covered oaks and is eminently more playable. Located 50 minutes from Hilton Head Island.

Hilton Head National
Visually pleasing, but not too terribly challenging Gary Player daily-fee course. Tight fairways demand keen accuracy. Greens are mildly undulating; holes 9 and 18 share a double green. Well maintained, despite heavy play. An enjoyable course for all ability levels. Home of the Jimmy Ballard Golf Workshop. Hosted the Amoco-Centel Championship in 1991, an "over-40" PGA-approved tournament won by Jim Thorpe.

Island West Golf Club
Scenic marshside course with elevated tees, rolling fairways and no forced

carries. Challenging, yet highly playable with "safe" routes for the cautious. The back nine is particularly strong. An enjoyable course for the good player, and very accommodating for the mid- to high handicappers.

Old South G.L.

Outstanding new course that ranks among the Southeast's finest daily fee layouts, thanks to a breathtaking setting. Front nine rolls through densely wooded forests with some intriguing marsh holes, but the back nine ranks among the best in the Hilton Head area. Several holes skirt the marsh and offer a superb test as well as magnificent views. Architect Clyde Johnston, who is also responsible for the fine Heather Glen and Ocean Harbour courses in Myrtle Beach, preserved the beauty of the land while creating a fine test of golf. A definitive "must-play" in the area.

Oyster Reef G.C.

One of the island's most formidable tests, particularly from the tips. Course was named as one of the country's outstanding new courses in 1983. Rolling fairways, many doglegs, extensive bunkering and undulating greens. Par-3 sixth hole, which plays against a backdrop of Port Royal Sound, is one of the island's most photographed holes. Plans call for the course to eventually become private.

Robert Cupp Course, Palmetto Hall Plantation

Innovative new course originally designed by Cupp on computer, resulting in lots of geometric shapes, sharp lines, and angles. A demanding test from the tips—featuring the highest slope rating in the Lowcountry—with many long, forced carries. But it's much more playable from the forward tees.

Rose Hill C.C.

Gently rolling course with tight fairways bordered by thick stands of magnolias, live oaks and towering pines. Liberal bunkering and mildly undulating greens. Newer West Nine features a 600-yard par-5, but all in all, this is a very playable country club-type course.

THE

The 8th hole on the Marshside nine of the Sea Island Golf Club.

GOLDEN ISLES

The Golden Isles

The Complete List of Courses Open to the Public

Location	Course	Address
Jekyll Island	Jekyll Island—	
	Indian Mound	322 Wylly Rd.
	Oceanside	322 Wylly Rd.
	*Oleander	322 Wylly Rd.
	Pine Lakes	322 Wylly Rd.
St. Simons Island	*The Hampton Club	1 Tabby Shore
	Sea Palms (27)	5445 Frederica Rd.
	*St. Simons Island Club	100 Kingsway
	*Sea Island G.C. (36)	100 Retreat Ave.

* Recommended Course ** Highly Recommended

THERE IS PERHAPS NO OTHER REGION IN THE U.S. THAT WEARS ITS heritage more proudly, and more authentically, than the strand of tiny barrier islands along Georgia's southeastern coast. The Golden Isles, as they as known, portray a heritage of graciousness and style that has sadly been lost throughout much of the South.

Poets and storytellers have been drawn to the tranquil beauty of the region for more than 100 years, and historians are fascinated by the events that have taken place along these marshy lowlands. The invitingly mild year-round weather has made the Golden Isles a popular vacation destination since the turn of the century and while growth has been inevitable, a profound sense of history lingers in every breeze that whisps across the vast salt marshes.

Flags of five different nations have flown along the Golden Isles and around Brunswick, Ga., the historic port town that serves as the gateway to the islands from busy Interstate 95. The Spanish flag was first raised over Georgia by Hernando de Soto around 1540, as soldiers came seeking gold and missionaries came seeking religious converts among the Indians. The French ruled briefly in the mid-1500s as Jean Ribault sought to establish a haven for French Huguenots, but the Spanish soon regained control and reigned until 1736, when General James Edward Oglethorpe established Fort Frederica on St. Simons and ushered in an era of English dominance that lasted until the outbreak of the Revolutionary War.

Slope/Rating: Men	Women	Par	Cost	Phone
69.7/124	70.0/122	72	Low	(912) 635-2368
69.6/123	70.3/123	72	Low	(912) 635-2170
70.0/124	70.3/123	72	Low	(912) 635-2368
70.0/126	71.9/124	72	Low	(912) 635-2368
69.2/120	69.9/120	72	High	(912) 634-0255
69.2/124	70.9/119	72	Moderate	(912) 638-3351
70.1/130	70.0/124	72	Moderate	(912) 638-5130
70.9/130	72.9/126	72	Very High	(912) 638-5118

The antebellum era flourished prior to the war, as sea island cotton became king and sprawling plantations operated all along the Georgia coast. When Georgia joined its southern sister states in seceding from the Union in 1861, the Confederate "stars and bars" flew here until the war's end in 1865. In the late 1880s, a group of the world's wealthiest families— Rockefellers, Vanderbilts, Morgans, Pulitzers, and others—established Jekyll Island as their winter retreat, and the Golden Isles entered into a new era as a unspoiled, tranquil seaside destination.

The other islands in the Golden Isle chain soon became equally popular, though still largely accessible to only a privileged few. Timber magnate Philip Berolzheimer bought Little St. Simons Island as his family's private hunting and fishing preserve in 1908; today, the 10,000-acre island is run by Berolzheimer's descendants as a small, rustic retreat. In 1928, automaker Howard Coffin—the man who invented the Hudson— established The Cloister on Sea Island and began the traditions for which the hotel and the island have become world famous.

Tourism has since become the industry of record for the Golden Isles. The state of Georgia took over Jekyll Island in 1946 and has restored much of its historical grandeur while adding a wide range of accommodations, amenities (including 63 holes of golf) and other leisure-oriented activities. Sea Island and St. Simons Island have both become renowned golf destinations. And the smaller islands—Little St. Simons and

Cumberland—offer limited accommodations in still largely undeveloped settings.

The Golden Isles offer much more than the typical seaside destinations. The area is steeped in rich history, spell-binding beauty and an unmatched tranquility. The people of the region carry on age-old traditions and pass on fascinating stories and laughable legends, all the while providing guests with all the modern comforts. The allure of the Golden Isles is unavoidable, and if the twisting, moss-draped live oaks could talk, they'd tell you to stick around for awhile.

Getting There

Brunswick and the Golden Isles of Georgia are situated on Georgia's southeast Atlantic coast, approximately 75 miles from Savannah, 65 miles from Jacksonville, Fla., and 280 miles from Atlanta. Access by car is by I-95, U.S. Highways 17 and 341, and Georgia Highways 82 and 520. Brunswick's Glynco Jetport is served by regular flights of Atlantic Southeast Airlines (ASA/Delta Connection). Private pilots may use Glynco Jetport, McKinnon Airport on St. Simons Island or Jekyll Island Airport. For boaters, the Golden Isles are located along the Intracoastal Waterway, and there are numerous full-service marinas in the area.

Weather

The gentle ocean breezes help warm the winters and cool the summers of the Golden Isles, thus providing for mild year-round weather. The annual average temperature is 68 degrees, while the annual average rainfall is approximately 50 inches. Typically, July and August are the warmest months (average highs of 89 degrees) while December and January are the coolest (average highs of 62 degrees, lows of 43 degrees).

Activities

Bicycling around the Golden Isles is perhaps the best way to experience the area's abundant natural beauty; St. Simons Island and Jekyll Island both offer several rental services, as do the major resort properties. Another popular outdoor activity is horseback riding, with Sea Island Stables on St. Simons providing guided tours and trail rides. There are a number of tennis facilities open to the public throughout the islands, with the majority of public-access courts located on Jekyll Island. Island Tours on St. Simons offers daily guided tours of the area by land or sea, and sightseeing cruises are offered out of Brunswick, St. Simons, Sea Island, and Jekyll. For fishing, there are public-access piers in Brunswick, St. Simons and Jekyll, and charter expeditions are available from marinas on all the major islands. Day-trippers will want to make the hour's drive north to historic Savannah or to Waycross, the home of the famous

Okefenokee Swamp. Exploring Cumberland Island, the tiny barrier island just south of Jekyll, is another great way to spend the day; make sure to take a picnic lunch.

Attractions

Brunswick: Old Town National Register District, several streets and squares in the southern section of town lined with old homes noted for their turn-of-the-century architecture; Overlook Park, a fine vantage point for viewing the vast and beautiful marshlands and river network that flank Brunswick and much of coastal Georgia. **St. Simons Island:** The Museum of Coastal History and St. Simons Lighthouse, the restored 1872 lighthouse keeper's home and the towering 106-foot lighthouse; Bloody Marsh Battle Site, the historic grounds where in July 1742, an outnumbered force of British troops ambushed and defeated Spanish troops, halting an attack of Fort Frederica and marking the turning point in the Spanish invasion of Georgia; Fort Frederica National Monument, built by General Oglethorpe in 1736 and offering historic films, informative talks and tours, and soldier/colonial life programs in summer; Christ Church, Frederica, where John and Charles Wesley, the fathers of American Methodism, first preached to the natives beneath the limbs of an enormous oak tree. **Jekyll Island:** The Historic District Orientation Center, with slide presentations on the island's history and tram tours of the "Millionaires Row," the wonderfully preserved winter homes of the Rockefellers, Morgans, Vanderbilts, and other prominent families who wintered here.

Shopping

Brunswick: The downtown area is undergoing a major revitalization aimed at restoring the Victorian atmosphere, with numerous retailers, antique shops and restaurants all within walking distance of each other. There's also Glynn Place Mall, with 100 retail shops, services, restaurants as well as a hotel and miniature golf course. **St. Simons Island:** The Village on the island's southern end features a large cluster of shops and restaurants; further north are countless stores and boutiques located at Demere Village, Retreat Village, Redfern Village, Longview Shopping Center, Hanover Square, and Frederica Walk North. Golden Isles Marina Village, located on the St. Simons causeway, offers dining and shopping in a beautiful river-edge setting overlooking the marina.

For More Information

Brunswick & The Golden Isles Visitors Bureau, 4 Glynn Avenue, Brunswick, GA 31520, (800) 933-COAST; (912) 265-0620.

Popular Dining Options

Jekyll Island: *The Grand Dining Room, Jekyll Island Club,* excellent steaks and fresh seafood in an elegant setting with crystal wall lamps and a pillared fireplace, all-day dining; *Blackbeard's,* ocean views and hearty portions of fresh local seafood and cooked-to-order steaks, outdoor dining in season; and *Zachry's Seafood House,* seafood specialties from their own shrimp boat, as well as steak and chicken and a very good salad bar, very casual. **St. Simons Island:** *Alfonza's Olde Plantation Supper Club,* gracious and relaxed atmosphere with seafood, superb steaks and southern fried chicken; *Emmeline and Hessie,* fresh seafood (great specialty shrimp dishes) overlooking the Intracoastal Waterway and St. Simons Bay, also homemade soups, sauces and baked goods; *Blanche's Courtyard,* casual Victorian setting with fresh, Lowcountry seafood specialties and hand-cut steaks, weekend entertainment; and *The Crab Trap,* hole-in-the-wall atmosphere with superb seafood (fried and broiled) with all the trimmings, very casual and no credit cards accepted.

THE RESORTS IN DEPTH

The Cloister
"The Classic Sea Island Retreat"

Chances are, even if you've been a regular guest at The Cloister on Sea Island, you've probably never ridden a horse through the surf, or shot skeet at the range over the marsh, or gone fishing. You've probably never ridden a bike underneath the canopy of Spanish moss-draped oaks, or hung out by the pool, or had a massage, or danced until the wee hours.

In fact, all you've probably ever done at The Cloister is eat, sleep and play golf. In some ways, that's a shame. But then again, it's not unusual. While some people go to The Cloister for those other fine things, others return again and again for the golf (and the food – let's not forget the food). But the fact remains that people do go back, again and again. Generation after generation. And that, probably more than anything else, helps define why The Cloister sits regally on her throne as one of the queens of American resorts. Whatever it is that The Cloister does, it does it well enough to bring people back.

Previously known as Fifth Creek Island, Isle of Palms, Long Island,

The seventh hole on Sea Island's Plantation Nine. Plantation has been renovated several times over the years, including a redesign by H.S. Colt and C.H. Alison in 1929, and a complete overhaul in 1992 supervised by Rees Jones.

Glynn Island and Sea Island Beach, it was a relatively uninhabited Sea Island that Ohio auto magnate Howard Coffin found back in 1924, when the first rude causeway was built over the inlets and salt marshes that separate the Golden Isles from Brunswick, Ga., on the mainland. Coffin thought this pretty stretch of beach would make for a good resort, and hired well-known resort architect Addison Mizner to do the drawings. In 1928, Mizner's Mediterranean-style stucco and tile hotel was finished, and The Cloister opened. He built oversized public areas, broad expanses of law, and a plethora of flower beds to give the place an elegant look.

Along with his cousin, Alfred W. Jones, Sr., Coffin formed the Sea Island Company to operate the hotel, and also bought up a great deal of real estate on both Sea Island and neighboring St. Simons Island. That economic investment, and the fact that the Jones family has been in control for the last 60 years, have both contributed to the ongoing success of the enterprise.

During the "Roaring Twenties," golf was booming, so the first order of business was to build the guests a nice place to play. The site selected was the former Retreat Plantation, a pre-Colonial cotton plantation about five miles down the road on St. Simons Island. Back in 1736, several new varieties of cotton seedlings were imported from the Caribbean island of Anguilla. After some selective growing a strain called Sea Island cotton

Above left: A year before he built Doral's Blue Monster, Dick Wilson completed the Retreat nine at The Cloister, including this finishing ninth hole guarded by bunkers and live oaks. Below: Part of Sea Island's challenge are the daunting approaches over the water.

became known as a particularly high-quality variety. You can still buy shirts made of Sea Island cotton, which today is mostly grown in Egypt.

The entrance drive to the golf club is framed by two lines of sentinel live oaks, while the clubhouse was built around an old barn. The tabby remnants of the plantation's slave hospital still remain today.

Walter Travis built the first golf holes on the former plantation site, but two years later the English firm of Colt and Alison were hired to rework Travis' nine and build nine more. The Plantation Nine and the Seaside Nine were thus opened in 1929. Dick Wilson designed the Retreat Nine in 1960, and Joe Lee added the Marshside Nine in 1973 using the plantation's old mule road across the marsh as a base for three rather narrow holes.

It should be noted that these golf holes were not commissioned with the

idea of testing the finest professional golfers of the day. The Sea Island Golf Club is resort golf at its finest. It was designed for relaxed and sporting golf, with a mixture of fun-and-easy holes and several real attention-getters. This is not to say that the golf is a pushover—it rarely is. The wind off the nearby ocean is always a factor of some sort, and occasionally an evil one. There are plenty of bunkers around, and lagoons, creeks, and marshland all come into frequent play.

The Seaside Nine, which seem to be favorite of long-time guests, boasts two fine par-four holes, the fourth and the seventh. Both call for heroic carries off the tee over the serpentine wanderings of a creek bounded by marshgrass. And since they go in opposite directions, one of them is normally played directly into a headwind. The seventh, at 424 yards, is the most photographed and often cursed at the 19th hole. Bold players will try to blast one down the left side, flirting with the creek, a shot that requires a carry of more than 200 yards. If properly executed, this strategy is rewarded with an open look to the green. Less daring players will opt for the safe tee shot down the right, leaving a long iron to a green which is completely hidden behind two mammoth, high-lipped fairway bunkers.

The Retreat Nine features fairways narrower than most and guarded by stands of imposing oaks. If you're driving the ball sideways, you will get plenty of practice on your low punch shots. Yet many consider the Marshside Nine—a Joe Lee design—to be the toughest of the four layouts, particularly if the sea breezes are up. With the exception of the first and last holes, every mis-hit shot on this nine is in real danger of finding a watery grave.

The weakest of the four venues used to be the oldest, the Plantation Nine. But no longer. In the spring of 1992 the bulldozers moved in and began reworking the original Walter Travis layout, with plans drawn by noted architect Rees Jones. All nine greens were rebuilt to USGA standards, the course was lengthened, and Jones added considerably to its strategic difficulties.

Guests can also play the St. Simons Island Club, another Joe Lee layout a mile down the road from the Sea Island Golf Club. After the first two or three holes on this 6,490-yard track, you get the impression that this is a benign little layout. Then the fairways narrow, black lagoons lurk everywhere, and with your ball being blown around by the wind off the nearby shore, one's opinion often takes a somewhat nastier turn.

Then again, there is probably no better place in the country for your game to go sour. The Golf Learning Center at the Sea Island Golf Club is one of the finest facilities anywhere for working on your game. The center is home to a *Golf Digest* Instruction School headed by senior instructor Jack Lumpkin. Inside the building is an array of video equipment used to analyze your swing. Outside are hundreds of feet of hitting areas—including some protected against rain—chipping and pitching greens, practice bunkers and putting greens. Golf schools run year-round, with accommodations at The Cloister. The Sea Island Golf Club staff also offers lessons, and there's a club-fitting shop right off the practice tee.

The Cloister is known in some southern circles as the summer home of the yuppie set, and The Cloister's programs for children are indeed without equal. From early in the morning until after dinner, kids are entertained, educated and enlivened by an energetic staff of fresh-faced college students.

The Cloister is one of the last resorts that offers the full American Plan. The main dining room is top drawer all the way. Elegant surroundings—

linen, china and silver—often mask food that pretends to be equally impressive, but The Cloister's kitchen consistently delivers. The menu changes daily, and while fresh seafood is a mainstay, there's always good local game on the menu as well. The Sunday night buffet is an absolute must, and if you don't try the seafood gumbo or the fresh baked cornbread they may revoke your golf privileges.

Dressing up is *de rigueur.* Coat and tie are required for gentlemen, dresses for ladies. Even the kids have to be spit-shined and polished. On Wednesday and Saturday nights black tie and evening gowns are recommended, although still optional. After dinner the ballroom across the hall livens up, and with the live orchestra playing until late into the night, one can conjure up all kinds of Gatsby-esque imagery.

There are alternatives to the dress-up set; for example, the nightly seafood buffet offered at the Beach Club. Coats and ties are not required, and there are always three or four deep-water treasures from which to choose. Guests can also dine informally at either of the golf clubhouses.

Friday nights are extra special. Guests are shuttled in a Jeep convoy out to Ocean Grove at the tip of Sea Island for a plantation supper, kind of a high-end barbecue. The waves lap against the beach, the stars twinkle, and the band plays Caribbean favorites. If you can stand the sight of the honeymooners overcome by the romance of its all and smooching underneath the tiki lamps, you'll find more good food than is probably legal.

When George and Barbara Bush returned for their second honeymoon at The Cloister a few years ago, they booked a suite in the Harrington House on the beach. A good choice, but there are equally nice rooms in the Retreat and Hamilton Houses on the beach or the River House. The families who return every summer seem to like the guest houses scattered around the flower-bedecked grounds.

If one still doubts that The Cloister is the last stronghold of Southern gentility and manners, all doubts will be erased upon check-out. The Cloister accepts no credit cards, and not only welcomes your personal check, but will, if you wish, send you the bill after you get home. It's an enduring and endearing symbol of the trust that guests at The Cloister are part of the family.

Jekyll Island
"Where Aristocracy Took A Holiday"

It is utterly intoxicating to walk on the very turf where the Rockefellers, Morgans and Vanderbilts held lawn parties, dabbled at croquet, hunted wild boar, chased par, and simply had a good time being rich. A certain smugness consumes the mere mortal as he freely floats about the grounds the fabulously affluent rigidly kept to themselves, a place that was off-limits to all but the small membership of an intensely exclusive club. There should be a sign that reads: "Welcome to Jekyll Island - Now It's Your Turn."

Indeed, visitors to Jekyll Island, a little sliver of land off the Georgia coast, can still get a taste of what it was like some 90 years ago, when America's super-industrialists came to unwind from the rigors of capitalism. A pristine croquet lawn still fronts the grand, turreted hotel. The original links still challenge the golfer. And most of the immense "cottages"—so referred to by people who regarded anything under 80,000 square feet as quaint—still stand. While Jekyll Island long ago went public, you can still peer into the ultra-private world that was, a world that belonged to an envied few for whom the American Dream came true.

It was in 1855 that an entrepreneur named John Eugene du Bignon decided to turn Jekyll Island into a hunting retreat for the country's movers and shakers; du Bignon, who had inherited a parcel of Jekyll from his family (a long line of cotton growers) acquired the entire island for $13,100. The following year the Jekyll Island Club was formed, with

Dick Wilson knew how to make a tough hole, and this number one handicap, par-5, 561-yard 4th hole at Jekyll's Oleander shows how a good one can begin, with a sharp dogleg-right, and how one can finish with this severely trapped approach to the green with water in play.

membership limited to 100.

It wasn't long before the palmetto-studded barrier island evolved into much more than a hunting preserve. Jekyll became the winter retreat for moguls and their broods. America's fanciest families journeyed from their northern estates, bringing with them armies of servants and mountains of trunks. Some traveled by private rail cars, others by 300-foot-long steamer yachts. Horse-drawn carriages transported new arrivals to their cottages, none of which had kitchens. Members were expected to be sociable and have their repasts at the club (now the hotel).

Jekyll Island was such a self-contained realm that it had its own oyster bed, terrapin pens, dairy farm and vegetable garden. A taxidermist stuffed and mounted game bagged by the club's hunters. At the infirmary, doctors from Johns Hopkins University treated common colds and toothaches. At a tiny red-cedar church - Faith Chapel - services were held under open beams and the gaze of gargoyles. Light streamed in through two elaborate stained-glass windows, one of which was wrought by L.C. Tiffany.

At the turn of the century, golf was still a novelty in this country. Yet while golf was hardly the "cats meow," to use the vernacular of the day, the Jekyll Island Club carved links out of sand dunes near the beach in 1898. When club members weren't poring over their bridge hands, playing billiards, tracking down wildlife, taking tea or lounging in 500-pound stuffed-leather couches, smoking hand-rolled Cuban cigars and perusing *The New York Times*, they were out on verdant sweeps of grass, doing what would frustrate generations to come - playing golf.

But all good things come to an end, so some wise, if cynical philosopher once said. The Jekyll Island Club had its inevitable demise, as the Great Depression destroyed a number of its key members. But economical reversal was not the sole contributor to this little kingdom's downfall. The off-spring of the wealthy were beginning to look upon Jekyll Island as a somewhat stuffy place to spend a holiday. Jekyll had lost its sparkle. The final blow came in 1941, when the United States entered World War II. A scarcity of supplies and labor, which were being delivered to the war effort, forced the club to close, temporarily at first, then permanently, thus ending an epoch era in the South.

More than 50 years later, Jekyll Island, now owned by the state of Georgia, is a whole different scene. Today, Jekyll is everyman's playground. Accommodations run the gamut from a Comfort Inn to the tony Jekyll Island Club Hotel, which, with the aid of $17 million, has been restored to its original resplendence.

Regular scheduled tours through the island's historic district provide visitors with intimate glimpses into the lives of yesterday's millionaires.

Wild turkey and deer may sometimes be seen on this par-5, 534-yard, par-5 15th hole on Jekyll Island's Pine Lakes Course.

There are lush, moss-shrouded picnic grounds and campsites. There's the Jekyll Island Fitness Center, 13 fast-dry clay tennis courts, and enough miniature golf to keep the kids happy.

For serious stuff, there are 63 regulation holes. In fact, Jekyll Island is the largest golf resort in Georgia. Lush fairways snake through a relatively flat landscape punctured with palmettos, live oak, pines, yucca, pampas, oleander and jungles of wild grape vines. Playing golf on Jekyll Island is as much a nature walk as a sporting activity. Wild turkeys scramble through the rough, an alligator rises in one of the water hazards, red-tail hawks and blue heron perch on tree stumps. (This is one of the few

barrier islands that is still a nesting site for the huge loggerhead turtle).

It was on Jekyll Island that Andy Bean learned to hit a golf ball a country mile. His father was the club professional here 20 years ago. Young Bean spent a lot of time on the 18-hole Oleander stretch, the longest of Jekyll's courses at 6,241 yards from the white tees. You can let loose on these wide fairways, but beware the water, which is plentiful and insidious. Wind is also a major factor on the Oleander course, especially on the par-four 12th hole, where the golfer always plays into a stiff breeze off the ocean.

The Pine Lakes course serves up tight corridors of pines that keep you on the straight and narrow—if you're smart, that is. Play it safe off the tee, and you'll get home with your self respect intact. Particularly treacherous is the 400-yard, par-4 fourth, a hole so narrow it's downright claustrophobic.

The Indian Mound course is a bit of an antidote to any pain the golfer might have suffered on Jekyll's other tracks. Short and sweet, it was built with one objective: to move people around...fast. The only real agitation this stretch might cause is encountered on the par-four 13th, where the opening to a tiered, bunker-guarded green seems as small as the eye of a needle.

The nine-hole Oceanside layout is what remains of Jekyll's first 18-hole golf course. This is a wicked little number, characterized by tiny greens and hard-to-negotiate sand dunes (there were no bulldozers in the late 1800s). On the par-5 fifth hole, dubbed the "Mae West," the golfer is compelled to drive between two voluptuous sand dunes. Fly over the left dune and you might as well be blindfolded for your second shot.

The Oceanside stretch is often referred to as the "millionaires' course;" one more landmark on Jekyll Island, one more place where you can inhale the pine- and salt-scented air and drift back to a time when wealth, power and gentility converged on an obscure strip of earth off the Georgia coast.

The King & Prince Beach Resort

"The Crown Jewel of St. Simons Island"

It began more than 50 years ago as a beach club for those seeking private tranquility on the southeastern shore of St. Simons Island. Yet while the King & Prince Beach Resort has grown in size and stature to become the island's finest oceanfront retreat, much of the opulence of the club's halcyon days remains intact.

That's not to say, however, that snobbery prevails at the King & Prince. Far from it. This is a magnificent family-oriented destination, with an amenity base comparable to much larger, glitzier resorts and a laid-back atmosphere that not only encourages, but demands relaxation. To borrow from popular phraseology, if you can't chill here, you can't chill anywhere.

The allure of the King & Prince has been substantially enhanced in recent years by the development of Hampton Plantation, a 300-acre private residential community on the northern tip of St. Simons Island. The connection is golf...great golf. The Hampton Club features a tantalizing 18-hole golf course, designed by Joe Lee, that is accessible to King & Prince guests. In fact, the hotel offers some excellent packages that include all the perks of the King & Prince as well as unlimited golf at Hampton.

Strange bedfellows, you might think, a thriving oceanfront resort and a small, private residential community. It seems that the owners of the King & Prince had a half-interest in the development of Hampton Plantation. Allowing hotel guests to secure starting times at an otherwise private course substantially elevated the King and Prince's stature among golfers. The cash flow generated from the outside play enabled Hampton to operate smoothly in the face of fluctuating real estate sales. And Hampton club members accepted this encroachment on their facility, because it kept their dues and assessments lower.

The result? Everybody wins, save perhaps for the golfer who can't count "control" among the attributes of his game. Hampton Club measures just 6,465 yards from the tips and an even 6,000 from the regular tees, and if you don't have the sense to keep your driver in the bag and your ball in the fairway, you probably deserve to contribute a dozen or so to the surrounding marshlands.

From a design standpoint, Hampton Club has two highly memorable sets of holes. The first set is Nos. 3, 4 and 5, two par-fives and a par-three that play around an L-shaped lake and border an absolutely stunning 12-mile expanse of salt marsh. Another hole on the front side that deserves mention is the ninth, a 365-yard, dogleg-left par-four. The fairway is 40 yards wide, the green is 45 yards deep, and depending on your tee shot and the pin placement, the approach can require anything from 8-iron to 4-wood, over water.

There is an incomparable sense of anticipation surrounding play on the second set of memorable holes at Hampton Club. Without question, holes 12 through 15 are some of the most awe-inspiring tests of golf in Georgia.

The Hampton Club, pictured above, is home to several of the most picturesque holes in the Golden Isles.

George Cobb, who built the earliest courses on Hilton Head Island, designed the two original nines at Sea Palms, including this 4th hole on the Tall Pines nine. Below: Superb views and difficult carries are the risk and reward of a marshland course, of which The Hampton Club (pictured here) is an excellent example.

They were created on four, small natural islands that run perpendicular to the western shore of the property, an effort that required Lee to work in concert with the Georgia Department of Natural Resources. His construction team's first challenge was to provide access to the islands by building over 800 feet of elevated cart bridges. Then they had to accommodate the limited load capacity of the bridges by devising methods of transporting equipment and materials over to the islands.

Suffice to say, they pulled it off. The first two islands serve as the tee and green, respectively, for the par-three 12th, a fiesty 118-yarder. The third island is the tee for the No. 13, a 386-yard par-4, while the fourth island contains the 13th fairway and all of Nos. 14 (461 yards, par 5) and 15 (155 yards, par 3). Any further description of these holes would betray their incomparable beauty. You have to be there.

And you should. Spend some time at the King & Prince, in a room overlooking the outdoor pool or the ocean or in a two- or three-bedroom beach villa. Enjoy the magnificent dining of the Delegal Room (the Sunday brunch is requisite); retreat to the quiet confines of the Solarium with a good book or to the Reading Room for a round of bridge, or scout for historical relics along the resort's wide expanse of private beach. By all means, play a few rounds at Hampton Club. And, just for fun, you can pretend that you've discovered the best-kept secret of the Golden Isles.

Sea Palms Golf & Tennis Resort
"A Sleeping Giant Awakens on Historic St. Simons"

Chances are, if you live anywhere north of the Mason-Dixon line, Sea Palms Golf & Tennis Resort probably doesn't spring to mind as one of the premier golf destinations in the South. Yet while obscurity certainly has its place at Sea Palms, it may soon be a thing of the past for the 800-acre Four-Star/Four-Diamond resort and residential community that straddles Frederica Road, the scenic main drag on St. Simons Island.

For many years, St. Simons was known mostly as a historically rich island situated between Interstate 95 and swanky Sea Island. But thanks to some crafty management and marketing efforts by Interstate Hotels Corporation—the firm manages 46 full-service hotels across the U.S. including the Marriott at Sawgrass— and some magnificent new resort facilities, Sea Palms is enjoying a pleasant "coming out" of sorts over the past couple of years. A homey little retreat, long overshadowed by its more distinguished neighbors in the Golden Isle chain, Sea Palms has moved up to the big leagues.

Over and above all else, Sea Palms prides itself on its golf: 27 holes of good, clean fun. There is no man-made trickery here; no blind shots, no pot bunkers, no 600-yard double-dogleg par-fives. Great Oaks is the longest of the nines at 3,405 yards from the back tees; Tall Pines measures 3,253 yards from the tips; and Sea Palms West comes in just under 3,000 yards. All 27 holes meander through dense forests of sprawling, century-old live oaks, sky-high pines, and fragrant honeysuckle and muscadine. Great Oaks and Tall Pines skirt alongside the Marshes of Glynn, adding an extra degree of challenge to the marvelous scenery.

These are courses that you can't help but enjoy, and they're among the most naturally beautiful in the Golden Isles. Don't let the lack of distance fool you. There's plenty of trouble with the marsh and the woods and the water (8 of the 9 holes on Sea Palms West has water directly in play). The bottom line is this: If you can hit it straight, you can score at Sea Palms. If you don't hit it straight...well, watch your language.

Regardless of your golf game, you'll certainly speak in complimentary terms about Sea Palms' other amenities. The Sea Palms tennis facility, which includes 12 hard and clay courts, was recently added as a site for the Nick Bolletieri Tennis Academy. There's a health club and spa; two swimming pools; a new 25,000-square-foot clubhouse with a magnificent restaurant, Oglethorpe's, and lounge; and a new conference center with more than 7,500 square feet of meeting space. The accommodations are equally enticing and varied. There are golf course villas and townhomes tucked deep into the woods or overlooking the marsh; unique two-story Pedestal Homes situated along the marsh; or a variety of guest rooms and suites adjacent to the clubhouse. The combination seems to be working: Sea Palms enjoys a remarkably high return rate, with most visitors being either repeat guests or referrals.

Still, Interstate Hotels isn't content to rest on its resort's reputation. Shortly after assuming management of Sea Palms in July 1992, the company initiated several new marketing and advertising campaigns in Jacksonville and Atlanta—both of which have been integral markets for Sea Palms resort and real estate through the years. This new marketing push, coupled with the resort's new clubhouse and conference center, may finally bring Sea Palms something for which it is largely unaccustomed...notoriety.

Above: The 167-yard, par-3 6th hole at Jekyll Island's Oceanside nine, which was originally constructed in 1898 and later remodeled by Walter Travis.

Index of Resorts and Hotels

Note! Quoted rates represent the lowest available seasonal rates. They are typically based on double-occupancy, and will increase during the peak spring, summer, and fall seasons. Not all rates include local taxes, and gratuities. Also, high-profile courses may be available through hotel/resort packages at a significant surcharge. Be sure to confirm all rates before making any reservations.

NORTH CAROLINA MOUNTAINS

Maggie Valley Resort *340 Country Club Road, Maggie Valley, NC 28751 (800) 438-3861; (704) 926-1616.* RATES: Golf packages from $36 to $70 daily, depending on season and meal plan.

Waynesville Country Club *P.O. Box 390, Waynesville, NC 28786 (800) 627-6250; (704) 452-2258.* RATES: Golf packages from $59 to $80 daily, depending on season and meal plan.

High Hampton Inn & Country Club *562 Hampton Road, Cashiers, NC 28717. (800) 334-2551; In NC (800) 222-6954; (704) 743-2411.* RATES: Inn and cottage rooms from $75, including three meals daily. Green fees $19; carts, $20. Packages available.

Greystone Inn/Lake Toxaway Country Club *Greystone Lane, P.O. Box 6, Lake Toxaway, NC 28747 (800) 824-5766; (704) 966-4700.* RATES: Inn rooms from $196 to $306, including breakfast and dinner. Golf at Lake Toxaway C.C., $35; cart, $9.50.

Etowah Valley Country Club & Golf Lodge *P.O. Box 2150, Dept. 92 Hendersonville, NC 28793 (800) 451-8174; (704) 891-7022.* RATES: Golf packages from $69, including breakfast and dinner.

Grove Park Inn & Country Club *290 Macon Avenue, Asheville, NC 28804 (800) 438-5800; (704) 252-2711.* RATES: Guest rooms from $120 to $145. Discounted green fees for hotel guests. Packages available.

Great Smokies Hilton *1 Hilton Drive, Asheville, NC 28806 (704) 254-3211.* RATES: Guest rooms from $62 to $105, depending on season. Discounted green fees for hotel guests.

Esceeola Lodge/Linville Golf Club *Highway 221, Linville, NC 28646 (704) 733-4311.* RATES: Lodge rooms from $195 to $250, includes breakfast and dinner for two. Green fees at Linville G.C. $30; carts, $11 per person (guests rate).

PINEHURST AREA

Amble Inn Acres Bed & Breakfast *361 Alma Street, Vass, NC 28394 (919) 245-7175.* ACCOMMODATIONS: 3,500-square-foot home with four guest rooms and 2 1/2 baths; two guest rooms have private decks. AMENITIES: Private island with gazebo, one-mile nature trail, fishing and canoeing. RATES: Daily from $35 for non-golfers. No smoking.

Arborgate Inn *1408 Sandhills Boulevard, Aberdeen, NC 28315 (800) 722-7220; (919) 944-5633.* ACCOMMODATIONS: 80 guest rooms. AMENITIES: Swimming pool. RATES: Daily rates from $35 to $65, depending on package selected and time of year. Non-golfers, $36.95 daily.

Beacon Ridge Golf and Country Club *N.C. Highway 211, West End, NC 27376 (800) 762-1107; (919) 673-7700.* ACCOMMODATIONS: Golf villas with one- or two-bedroom suites and full kitchens. AMENITIES: Swimming pool, tennis courts, grill/lounge, 1,000-acre lake. RATES: Villas, three-day/two-night packages from $174 to $210.60. Non-golfer rates from $25. Single guest units from $67.

Best Western/Pinehurst Motor Inn *Sandhills Boulevard, Aberdeen, NC 28315 (800) 528-1234; (919) 944-2367.* ACCOMMODATIONS: 26 guest rooms. AMENITIES: Complimentary continental breakfast with daily newspaper delivery, outdoor pool. RATES: Daily rates from $105. Non-golfer rates from $42.95.5.

The Blacksmith Bed & Breakfast and Gallery *703 McReynolds, Carthage, NC 28327 (919) 947-1692.* ACCOMMODATIONS: Four guest rooms. AMENITIES: Full gourmet breakfast served in dining area or in private room. RATES: Daily rates from $30. Lunch and dinner served upon request at additional rates.

Condotels of Pinehurst *600 Highway 5, Pinehurst, NC 28374 (800) 255-4653; (919) 295-8008.* ACCOMMODATIONS: One-, two-, and three-bedroom fully furnished condominiums. RATES: Daily rates from $46. Vacation Rates (two-night minimum stay) from $68 daily, $408 weekly.

C.C. of Whispering Pines/Villas *2 Clubhouse Boulevard, Whispering Pines, NC 28327 (800) 334-9536; (919) 949-3777.* ACCOMMODATIONS: 32 inter-connecting guest rooms and nine condo-apartments. AMENITIES: Swimming pool and lake privileges. RATES: Three-day/two-night packages from $95.. Non-golfers, daily from $22.50.

Days Inn *1420 U.S. Highway 1 South, Southern Pines, NC 28387 (800) 325-2525; (919) 692-7581.* ACCOMMODATIONS: Standard guest rooms. AMENITIES: Color cable TV with HBO/ESPN, poolside bar and terrace, swimming pool, two restaurants, and live entertainment in J. Albert's Lounge. RATES: Three-day, two-night packages from $157. Non-golfers, $47.

Econo Lodge *U.S. Highway 1 South, Southern Pines, NC 28388 (919) 944-2324.* ACCOMMODATIONS: 91 standard guest rooms. AMENITIES: Swimming pool. RATES: Three-days/two-nights from $99; non-golfers, from $350.

The Fairway Motel *1410 U.S. Highway 1 South, Southern Pines, NC 28387 (919) 692-2711.* ACCOMMODATIONS: Standard guest rooms. AMENITIES: Enclosed swimming pool, sauna. RATES: Daily rates from $48; non-golfers from $32.

Foxfire Resort and Country Club *9 Foxfire Boulevard, Jackson Springs, NC 27281 (800) 736-9347; (919) 295-5555.* ACCOMMODATIONS: Golf course villas with fully equipped kitchens. AMENITIES: Tennis, fishing and swimming pool; restaurant and grill room; night putting green; lounge. RATES: Two-day/two-night packages from $151.

Hampton Inn *U.S. Highway 1 South, Southern Pines, NC 28387 (800) 333-9266; (919) 692-9266.* ACCOMMODATIONS: 126 standard guest rooms. AMENITIES: Outdoor swimming pool. RATES: Three-days/two-nights from $105; non-golfer from $38 per night.

The Holiday Inn *U.S. Highway 1 Bypass and Morganton Road, Southern Pines, NC 28388 (800) 262-5737; (919) 692-8585.* ACCOMMODATIONS: 160 guest rooms and suites. RATES: Three-days/two-nights from $204.50; non-golfers from $26.

The Holly Inn *Cherokee Road, Pinehurst, NC 28374 (800) 533-0041; In NC (800) 682-6901;*

(919) 295-2300. ACCOMMODATIONS: Guest rooms and suites. AMENITIES: Swimming pool, and dining on property. RATES: Available upon request. Two- and three-day packages available.

The Hotel Belvedere *120 W. Pennsylvania Avenue, Southern Pines, NC 28387 (919) 692-2240.* ACCOMMODATIONS: 35 guest rooms, suites and efficiencies RATES: Three-days/two-nights from $75; non-golfers from $30.95 daily.

Hyland Hills Resort *4110 U.S. Highway 1 North, Southern Pines, NC 28387 (919) 692-7615.* ACCOMMODATIONS: Standard guest rooms and efficiences. AMENITIES: Swimming pol.. RATES: Three days/ two-nights from $88; non-golfers from $17 daily.

Inn at the Bryant House *214 N. Poplar Street, Aberdeen, NC 28315 (919) 944-3300.* ACCOMMODATIONS: Inn rooms, efficiency apartment and guest cottage. RATES: From $45 daily.

The Inn at Eagle Springs *Samarcand Road, Eagle Springs, NC 27242 (919) 673-2722.* ACCOMMODATIONS: Five guest rooms. AMENITIES: Full breakfast served daily. RATES: From $50.

Longleaf Country Club *Midland Road, Pinehurst, NC 28374 (800) 522-9426; (919) 692-5522.* ACCOMMODATIONS: One- and two-bedroom fully furnished cottages. AMENITIES: 18-hole golf course designed by Dan Maples. RATES: Two days/two-nights from $285. Non-golfer rates and other packages available on request.

Magnolia Inn *Magnolia Road, Pinehurst, NC 28374 (800) 526-5562; (919) 295-6900.* ACCOMMODATIONS: Single and double guest rooms and suites. AMENITIES: Outdoor swimming pool; dining; English pub; tennis. RATES: Three-days/two-nights from $17; non-golfers from $60.

Midland Country Club/Knollwood Village *Midland Road, Pinehurst, NC 28374 (800) 633-8576; (919) 295-5011.* ACCOMMODATIONS: One-, two-, and three-bedroom condominiums and townhomes, and four-bedroom homes. AMENITIES: Restaurant; golf course. RATES: From $37.50; non-golfers from $35. Monthly rates from $875 to $1,350.

Mid Pines Resort *1010 Midland Road, Southern Pines, NC 28387 (800) CLARION; (919) 692-2114.* ACCOMMODATIONS: 118 rooms; 66 in the main hotel, 10 in the Lakeside Villas, and 42 in the Golf Course Villas. AMENITIES: 18 holes of golf (Donald Ross); 4 lighted tennis courts; swimming pool; dining room and lounge. RATES: From $26 (double) and $50 (single), European plan. Modified and Full American plans available.

Pine Cone Manor *450 East Philadelphia, Pinebluff, NC 28373 (919) 281-5307.* ACCOMMODATIONS: Bed-and-breakfast. AMENITIES: Whirlpool bath. RATES: From $35.

The Pine Crest Inn *Dogwood Road, Pinehurst, NC 28374 (919) 295-6121.* ACCOMMODATIONS: 40 inn rooms. AMENITIES: Four dining rooms with renowned cuisine; Mr. B's Old South Lounge with nightly entertainment at the piano bar. RATES: From $45, MAP.

Pinehurst Resort & Country Club *Highway 15/501 N., Pinehurst, NC 28374 (800) 334-9560; In NC (800) 672-4644.* ACCOMMODATIONS: 310 rooms at the Pinehurst Hotel; 49 rooms, suites, and parlors at the nearby Manor Inn; and the Golf Course and Lakeside condominiums with 140 one-, two- and three-bedroom condos with kitchens. AMENITIES: Seven 18-hole golf courses ; 24 tennis courts (four lighted); the Gun Club, nine trap and six skeet fields, sporting clays range, and tower shooting; Lake Pinehurst, restaurants, lounges. RATES: Golf package rates from $232.

The Pines Golf Resort *U.S. Highway 1 South, Pinebluff, NC 28373 (800) 334-4418; (919) 281-3165.* ACCOMMODATIONS: 40-room lodge, and two- and three-bedroom guest condominiums. AMENITIES: Swimming pool, three stocked fishing lakes, an 18-hole golf course, restaurant and grill.

RATES: Daily from $59. Non-golfers from $44.

Pine Needles Resort *Midland Rd., Southern Pines, NC 28387 (919) 692-7111.*
ACCOMMODATIONS: 71 rooms in 10 rustic, Swiss-style lodges. AMENITIES: 18 holes of golf
(Donald Ross); two grass tennis courts; health spa; outdoor swimming pool; main dining room and
separate 19th hole lounge. RATES: Spring and Fall seasons: From $105, Full American Plan.
Packages from $330. Summer and Winter seasons: From $59 for bed and breakfast, $85 for full
American Plan.

Woodlake Country Club *Star Rd., Vass, NC 28394 (800) 334-1126; (919) 245-4031.*
ACCOMMODATIONS: Two-bedroom townhomes. AMENITIES: 27-hole golf course designed by Ellis
and Dan Maples; restaurant and bar; two lighted tennis courts; 25-meter swimming pool; 1,130-acre
lake. RATES: 3-days/t2-nights from $162; non-golfers from $28 daily.

MYRTLE BEACH

Beach Colony Resort *5308 North Ocean Boulevard, Myrtle Beach, SC 29577 (800) 222-
2141; CANADA (800) 243-2141; (803) 449-4010.* ACCOMMODATIONS: Fully equipped oceanfront
suites. AMENITIES: Indoor and outdoor pools, racquetball court, tennis, restaurant and lounge.
RATES: Daily from $34.

Beach Cove Resort *Oceanfront at 48th Avenue South, North Myrtle Beach, SC 29582 (800)
331-6533; (803) 272-4044.* ACCOMMODATIONS: Oceanfront suites with private balconies.
AMENITIES: Indoor and outdoor pools, hot tubs, saunas, racquetball, dining,bar and lounge. RATES:
From $40 daily.

Best Western Landmark Resort Hotel *Oceanfront at 15th Avenue S., Myrtle Beach,
SC 29577 (800) 845-0658; (803) 448-9441.* ACCOMMODATIONS: Oceanview and oceanfront rooms.
AMENITIES: Heated swimming pool ; pub; restaurant; pool bar; sauna and steam room. RATES:
Singles from $49; golf widow rates from $28.

Blue Hawk on the Oceanfront *2801 South Ocean Boulevard, Myrtle Beach, SC 29577
(800) 331-7413; (803) 448-8488.* ACCOMMODATIONS: 80 two- and three-bedroom guest rooms,
efficiencies and condo units. AMENITIES: Two heated outdoor pools; and indoor whirlpool spa. RATES:
From $15 daily.

Bluewater Resort *2001 South Ocean Boulevard, Myrtle Beach, SC 29578 (800) 845-6994;
(803) 626-8345.* ACCOMMODATIONS: Efficiency apartments, executive suites, and two-bedroom
condos. AMENITIES: 70-foot indoor pool; four outdoor pools; five whirlpools; restaurant and lounge.
RATES: Villa packages from $25 daily.

The Breakers Resort Hotel/North Tower *Oceanfront at 21st and 27th Avenues
North, Myrtle Beach, SC 29578 (800) 845-0688; (803) 626-5000.* ACCOMMODATIONS: One-, two,
and three-bedroom suites with private balconies overlooking the ocean. AMENITIES: Indoor and
oceanfront pools and whirlpools; sauna; restaurant and lounge; tennis. RATES: From $34 daily.

The Caravelle Golf Resort & Villas *70th Avenue North, Myrtle Beach, SC 29572 (800)
845-0893; (803) 449-3331.* ACCOMMODATIONS: 420 standard rooms, suites and efficiences.
AMENITIES: Indoor and outdoor pools, whirlpools and sauna; restaurant. RATES: From $33 daily.

The Caribbean Motel & Villas *3000 North Ocean Boulevard, Myrtle Beach, SC 29577
(800) 845-0883; (803) 448-7181.* ACCOMMODATIONS: Oceanfront rooms and two- and three-
bedroom condominiums with kitchen, washer/dryer and separate living and dining areas. AMENITIES:

Outdoor pool and whirlpool, and restaurant. RATES: From $26 daily.

Carolina Winds *76th Avenue North, Myrtle Beach, SC 29578 (800) 523-4027; (803) 449-2477.* ACCOMMODATIONS: One-, two-, and three-bedroom condominiums. AMENITIES: Indoor and outdoor pools and whirlpools, saunas, and restaurant. RATES: From $36 daily.

Cherry Grove Manor *2104 North Ocean Boulevard, North Myrtle Beach, SC 29582 (800) 727-2322; (803) 249-2731.* ACCOMMODATIONS: One-, two-, and three-bedroom condominiums. AMENITIES: Oceanfront pool. RATES: Daily from $36.

Chesterfield Inn & Motor Lodge *700 North Ocean Boulevard, Myrtle Beach, SC 29578 (800) 392-3869; (803) 448-3177.* ACCOMMODATIONS: Standard guest rooms. AMENITIES: Outdoor pool, dining room. RATES: Six-day/six-night packages from $234.

The Clarion Resort at Sea Trail Plantation *650 Clubhouse Road, Sunset Beach, NC 28468 (800) 624-6601.* ACCOMMODATIONS: Fully furnished one- to four-bedroom villas and townhomes. AMENITIES: 54 holes of golf; swimming pool, sauna, whirlpool spa, lighted tennis; two full-service restaurants; two lounges. RATES: Mini-suites from $59 daily.

Compass Vacations *1610 Highway 17 South, North Myrtle Beach, SC 29582 (800) 624-6418; (803) 272-2073.* ACCOMMODATIONS: One-, two-, and three-bedroom oceanfront condominiums. AMENITIES: Indoor and outdoor pools, hot tubs, saunas, fully-equipped kitchens. RATES: Four-night/three-day packages from $109.

Condotels *North Myrtle Beach, SC; Surfside Beach, SC; Litchfield Beach, SC (800) 85CONDO; Canada (800) 845-0631.* ACCOMMODATIONS: Oceanfront and fairway condominiums. RATES: From $59 daily in September, $29 Winter and $39 Summer.

Coral Beach *1105 South Ocean Boulevard, Myrtle Beach, SC 29578 (800) 843-2684; (803) 448-8421.* ACCOMMODATIONS: Oceanview and oceanfront suites and efficiencies with fully equipped kitchens. AMENITIES: Two heated outdoor pools, three indoor whirlpools, steamroom and sauna restaurant, lounge, two snack bars, pool bar. RATES: Daily from $29.

Driftwood On-The-Oceanfront *16th Avenue North and the Oceanfront, Myrtle Beach, SC 29578(800) 942-3456; (803) 448-1544.* ACCOMMODATIONS: Oceanfront rooms and efficiencies. AMENITIES: Two oceanfront pools. RATES: From $26 daily.

Dunes Golf Villas *Atlantic Avenue, Garden City Beach, SC 29576 (800) 845-8191; (803) 651-2116.* ACCOMMODATIONS: One-, two- and three-bedroom oceanfront and oceanview condominiums with fully equipped kitchens. RATES: Two-bedroom condo, from $32.50 daily.

Dunes Village *5200 North Ocean Boulevard, Myrtle Beach, SC 29577 (800) 648-3539.* ACCOMMODATIONS: Oceanfront guest rooms. AMENITIES: Outdoor and indoor pools, hot water whirlpool, tennis courts, and coffee shop. RATES: From $33 daily.

Holiday Inn North *2713 Ocean Boulevard South, North Myrtle Beach, SC 29582 (800) 845-9700; (803) 272-6153.* ACCOMMODATIONS: Oceanfront guest rooms with private balconies. AMENITIES: Outdoor pool, restaurant and lounge with live entertainment. RATES: From $33 daily.

The Inn at Myrtle Beach *7300 North Ocean Boulevard, Myrtle Beach, SC 29572 (800) 845-0664; (803) 449-3361.* ACCOMMODATIONS: Oceanfront guest rooms, mini-suites, and efficiencies. AMENITIES: Heated outdoor pool, whirlpool, restaurant and lounge. RATES: From $89 daily.

Litchfield By-The-Sea *Pawleys Island, SC 29585 (800) 845-1897; (803) 237-3000.*

ACCOMMODATIONS: Hotel suites, golf cottages, and marshview, lakeview and oceanfront units available. AMENITIES: 3 golf courses; tennis; indoor and outdoor pools; racquetball, steam, sauna and whirlpool; restaurant and lounge; theatre; private beach. RATES: Suites and cottages daily from $29.

Myrtle Beach Hilton *10000 Beach Club Drive, Myrtle Beach, SC 29577 (800) 248-9228; (800) HILTONS; (803) 449-5000.* ACCOMMODATIONS: 392 oceanview and oceanfront guest rooms with private balconies. AMENITIES: Golf course; heated pools; four lighted tennis courts; and several restaurants and lounges. RATES: From $45 daily.

Myrtle Beach Martinique Resort & Conference Center *Oceanfront at 71st Avenue North, Myrtle Beach, SC 29578 (800) 542-0048; (803) 449-4441.* ACCOMMODATIONS: Oceanfront guest rooms. AMENITIES: Oceanfront pool, whirlpool and sundeck; indoor pool, whirlpool, saunas; restaurant and lounge with nightly entertainment. RATES: From $45 daily.

Ocean Dunes/Sand Dunes Resort & Villas *74th Avenue North, Myrtle Beach, SC 29572 (800) 845-6701; (803) 449-7441.* ACCOMMODATIONS: Oceanview and oceanfront guest rooms and villas. AMENITIES: Indoor/outdoor pools, saunas, whirlpools, steam rooms, racquetball, indoor driving range, two restaurants, two lounges, health and fitness center. RATES: From $58 daily.

The Palms *2500 North Ocean Boulevard, Myrtle Beach, SC 29578 (800) 528-0451; (803) 626-8334.* ACCOMMODATIONS: One-bedroom suites, two- and three-bedroom condominiums, and penthouses. AMENITIES: Indoor and outdoor oceanfront pools; Jacuzzis; outdoor whirlpool; saunas. RATES: From $33 daily.

Pan American Motor Inn *5300 N.Ocean Boulevard, Myrtle Beach, SC 29577 (800) 845-4501; (803) 449-7411.* ACCOMMODATIONS: Oceanfront guest rooms, efficiencies and 2-room apartments. AMENITIES: Indoor and outdoor pool, whirlpool, tennis, restaurant. RATES: From $33 daily.

Plantation Resort *1250 U.S. Highway 17 North, Surfside Beach, SC 29575 (800) 845-5039; (803) 238-3556.* ACCOMMODATIONS: Condominiums with kitchens washer/dryer. AMENITIES: Heated pool, whirlpool, saunas and steam rooms. RATES: From $30 daily.

Poindexter Golf Resort *1702 N. Ocean Boulevard, Myrtle Beach, SC 29577 (800) 248-0003; (803) 448-8327.* ACCOMMODATIONS: Standard oceanview and oceanfront guest rooms. AMENITIES: Three outdoor pools, indoor pool, Jacuzzis, restaurant. RATES: From $35 daily.

Radisson Resort at Kingston Plantation *9800 Lake Drive, Myrtle Beach, SC 29572 (800) 269-4300; (803) 449-0006.* ACCOMMODATIONS: One-bedroom oceanview suites; one-, two- and three-bedroom condos and villas. AMENITIES: Tennis, racquetball, indoor and outdoor pools, sauna and whirlpool, restaurant and lounge. RATES: From $45 daily.

Ramada Ocean Forest Resort *5523 North Ocean Boulevard, Myrtle Beach, SC 29577 (800) 522-0818; (803) 497-0044.* ACCOMMODATIONS: Oceanview and oceanfront suites with full kitchens; executive suites; and two-bedroom condos. AMENITIES: Indoor/outdoor pools, indoor whirlpool, steam room and sauna, pub and restaurant. RATES: From $30 daily.

Sea Crest Oceanfront *803 South Ocean Boulevard, Myrtle Beach, SC 29577 (800) 845-1112.* ACCOMMODATIONS: Standard and oceanfront rooms. AMENITIES: Pools, whirlpools, exercise room, mini-market, guest laundry, cafe and Pub. RATES: From $29 daily.

Sea Island - An Inn on the Beach *6000 N.Ocean Boulevard, Myrtle Beach, SC 29577 (800) 548-0767; (803) 449-6406.* ACCOMMODATIONS: Oceanfront standard rooms, efficiencies or deluxe rooms. AMENITIES: Heated pool, private beach, dining room. RATES: From $29 daily.

Sheraton Myrtle Beach Resort *Oceanfront at 2701 South Ocean Boulevard, Myrtle Beach, SC 29577 (800) 992-1055; (803) 448-2518.* ACCOMMODATIONS: Standard guest rooms. AMENITIES: Indoor and outdoor pools, whirlpool, restaurant and lounge. RATES: From $38 daily.

Southwind Villas *5310 North Ocean Boulevard, Myrtle Beach, SC 29577 (800) 842-1871; (803) 449-5211.* ACCOMMODATIONS: Fully furnished villas and townhouses. AMENITIES: Sauna, outdoor grills, 9-hole putting green. RATES: From $34 daily.

Tee & Sea Rentals and Management *P.O. Box 1093, Little River, SC 29566 (800) 845-6191; Canada (800) 458-4555; (803) 249-8572.* ACCOMMODATIONS: Golf course villas at Bay Tree and Tidewater Plantation. AMENITIES: Free swimming and tennis. RATES: From $44 daily.

The Winds Carriage House Inn *Oceanfront at 310 East First Street, Ocean Isle Beach, NC 28469 (800) 334-3581.* ACCOMMODATIONS: Oceanfront one- and two-bedroom suites, and four-bedroom Spa Houses with full kitchens, whirlpool spas, and separate bedrooms with full bath. AMENITIES: Heated pool; whirlpools; sauna. RATES: From $43 daily.

CHARLESTON

Kiawah Island Resort *P.O. Box 2941201, Charleston, SC 29412 (800) 654-2924; (803) 768-2121* ACCOMMODATIONS: 150 guest rooms and 330 villas of one- to four-bedrooms. AMENITIES: 72 holes of golf; two racquet clubs with 23 Har-Tru courts and 5 hard courts; 10 miles of beach; fishing; Straw Market shopping village, three restaurants, two lounges, bar. RATES: Available on request.

Seabrook Island Resort *1001 Landfall Way, Seabrook Island, SC 29455 (800) 845-2475; (803) 768-1000.* ACCOMMODATIONS: Fully furnished one-, two- and three-bedroom villas. AMENITIES: 36 holes of golf ; a 20-court tennis center; 3 1/2 miles of beach; an equestrian center; a swimming pool; three restaurants. RATES: Available upon request.

Wild Dunes Resort *P.O. Box 20575, Charleston, SC 29413 (800) 845-8880; (803) 886-6000.* ACCOMMODATIONS: One-, two-, and three-bedroom privately owned homes and villas overlooking the ocean, golf courses, tennis courts, lagoons and marshlands. AMENITIES: 36 holes of golf; racquet club with 17 Har-Tru courts (four lighted), two hard courts and a stadium court, 20 swimming pools, 2 1/2 miles of beach, two restaurants, snack bar. RATES: Villas from $130 daily.

HILTON HEAD ISLAND

Capuzello Vacations & Realty *P.O. Box 4866, Hilton Head Island, SC 29938 (800) 627-6545; (803) 785-7805.* ACCOMMODATIONS: Private homes, villas and hotel rooms. RATES: Two-night packages from $175 per person.

Crystal Sands Resort *130 Shipyard Drive, Hilton Head Island, SC 29928 (800) 334-1881; (803) 842-2400.* ACCOMMODATIONS: 331 guest rooms including 25 suites. AMENITIES: 27 holes of golf; 20-court racquet club; two swimming pools; two restaurants; a lounge/nightclub with live entertainment. RATES: Standard guest rooms from $140.

Fore & Shore Holidays of Hilton Head Island *P.O. Box 23574, Hilton Head Island, SC 29925 (800) 866-6336; (803) 681-2586.* ACCOMMODATIONS: Hotel rooms, golf villas and oceanfront condos. RATES: From $49 daily.

Hilton Head Island Hilton Resort *P.O. Box 6165, Hilton Head Island, SC 29938 (800)* *845-8001; (803) 842-8000.* ACCOMMODATIONS: 324 oversized guest rooms and suites. AMENITIES: Two swimming pools; two oceanside whirlpools; saunas, two restaurants, lounge, poolside bar. RATES: From $49 to daily. Two-night minimum stay required.

Hilton Inn on Hilton Head Island *12 Park Lane, Hilton Head Island, SC 29928 (800)* *852-0886; (803) 686-5700.* ACCOMMODATIONS: Hotel suites with fully equipped kitchen. AMENITIES: Outdoor heated swimming pool and hot tub with poolside bar; lighted tennis courts. RATES: Three-day, three-night packages from $267.

Hyatt Regency Hilton Head *P.O. Box 6167, Hilton Head Island, SC 29938 (800) 233-* *1234; (803) 785-1234.* ACCOMMODATIONS: 505 guest rooms including 31 suites and five ocean salons. AMENITIES: Indoor and outdoor pools, whirlpool, sauna and exercise room; shopping arcade, three restaurants, two lounges, poolside bar. RATES: From $80 daily.

Island Getaway *P.O. Box 5429, Hilton Head Island, SC 29938 (800) 476-4885; (803) 842-* *4664.* ACCOMMODATIONS: Homes and villas from one to six bedrooms. RATES: From $50 daily.

Lancaster Resort Rentals *P.O. Box 7887, Hilton Head Island, SC 29938* ACCOMMODATIONS: Private homes and villas, from one to six bedrooms. RATES: From $59 daily.

Oceanfront Rentals Company *11 New Orleans Road, Hilton Head Island, SC 29938* *(800) 845-6132; (803) 785-8161.* ACCOMMODATIONS: Homes and villas from one to seven bedrooms. RATES: From $55 daily.

Palmetto Dunes Resort *P.O. Box 5606, Hilton Head Island, SC 29938 (800) 845-6130;* *(803) 785-1161.* ACCOMMODATIONS: 500 rental homes and villas, from one to four bedrooms. AMENITIES: 54 holes of golf; racquet club with 28 courts; three miles of beach; 28 swimming pools; a wide variety of shops and restaurants; marina and harbor village. RATES: From $45 daily.

Sea Pines Resort *P.O. Box 7000, Hilton Head Island, SC 29938 (800) 845-6131; (803) 785-* *3333.* ACCOMMODATIONS: More than 500 rental villas and homes. AMENITIES: Three 18-hole golf courses; racquet club with 28 clay courts including a 10,000-seat stadium court; five miles of private beach; equestrian center; two marina villages with shopping and dining; many restaurants and lounges at Harbour Town marina, Sea Pines Center, and South Beach Marina. RATES: From $95 daily.

The Villas at the Westin Resort *2 Grasslawn Avenue, Hilton Head Island, SC* *29928(800) 933-3102; (803) 681-4000.* ACCOMMODATIONS: Two- and three-bedroom villas, fully equipped kitchens. RATES: Two-bedroom villas from $150, based on three-night minimum.

The Westin Resort *135 South Port Royal Drive, Hilton Head Island, SC 29928 (800) 228-* *3000; (803) 681-4000.* ACCOMMODATIONS: 410 guest rooms and 38 suites. AMENITIES: 36 holes of golf; 16 tennis courts of clay, hard and grass surfaces; three swimming pools; private beach; two restaurants, lounge, two poolside bars. RATES: From $175 daily.

GEORGIA'S GOLDEN ISLES

Best Western Jekyll Inn *975 North Beachview Drive, Jekyll Island, GA 31527 (800) 736-* *1064; (912) 635-2531.* ACCOMMODATIONS: 188 guest rooms; townhomes. AMENITIES: Pool, restaurant, bike rentals. RATES: From $49 daily.

Clarion Resort Buccaneer *85 South Beachview Drive, Jekyll Island, GA 31527 (800)*

CLARION; (912) 635-3230. ACCOMMODATIONS: 210 guest rooms. AMENITIES: Beach, swimming pool, tennis, restaurant, kitchenettes, RATES: From $55 daily.

The Cloister *Sea Island, Ga. 31561 (800) 732-4752 or (912) 638-3611.* ACCOMMODATIONS: 264 hotel rooms and suites. AMENITIES: 54 holes of golf; tennis; five miles of private beach; horseback riding; croquet, spa; four restaurants. RATES: From $131 daily.

Comfort Inn Island Suites *711 North Beachview Drive, Jekyll Island, GA 31527 (800) 221-2222; (912) 635-2211.* ACCOMMODATIONS: 178 suites. AMENITIES: Beach, swimming pool, restaurant , kitchenettes, bike rentals. RATES: From $55 daily

Days Inn Beach Resort *60 South Beachview Drive, Jekyll Island, GA 31527 (800) 325-2525; (912) 635-3319.* ACCOMMODATIONS: 162 guest rooms. AMENITIES: Beach, swimming pool, tennis, bike rentals, restaurant. RATES: From $39.95 daily.

Holiday Inn Beach Resort *200 South Beachview Drive, Jekyll Island, GA 31527 (800) 753-5955; (912) 635-3311.* ACCOMMODATIONS: 205 guest rooms; one- and two-bedroom villas AMENITIES: Beach, swimming pool, kitchenettes, tennis, restaurant. RATES: From $39 daily.

Jekyll Estates Inn *721 North Beachview Drive, Jekyll Island, GA 31527 (912) 635-2256.* ACCOMMODATIONS: Six guest rooms, 31 kitchenettes. AMENITIES: Beach, swimming pool, bike rentals, gift shop. RATES: From $48 daily.

Jekyll Island Club Hotel *371 Riverview Drive, Jekyll Island, GA 31527 (800) 333-3333; (912) 635-2600.* ACCOMMODATIONS: 134 guest rooms and suites. AMENITIES: Swimming pool, pool bar; croquet; tennis; private beach club; restaurant; deli/cafe/bakery. RATES: From $69 daily.

The King & Prince Beach Resort *P.O. Box 798, St. Simons Island, GA 31522 (800) 342-0212; (912) 638-3631.* ACCOMMODATIONS: 124 guest rooms and 38 villas. AMENITIES: 18 holes of golf; tennis; three swimming pools(one indoor); Jacuzzi; private beach; Solarium; Reading Room; restaurant and lounge. RATES: From $69 daily.

Ramada Inn *150 South Beachview Drive, Jekyll Island, GA 31527 (800) 835-2110; (912) 635-2111.* ACCOMMODATIONS: 110 guest rooms. AMENITIES: Beach, swimming pool, tennis, bike rentals, restaurant, lounge, meeting and convention facilities for up to 400. RATES: From $48 daily.

Seafarer Motel & Apartments *700 North Beachview Drive, Jekyll Island, GA 31527 (912) 635-2202.* ACCOMMODATIONS: 19 guest rooms, 48 apartments. AMENITIES: Beach, swimming pool, bike rentals, kitchenettes, restaurant and tennis within walking distance. RATES: From $49 daily.

Sea Palms Golf & Tennis Resort *5445 Frederica Road, St. Simons Island, GA 31522 (800) 841-6268; In GA (800) 282-1226; (912) 638-3351.* ACCOMMODATIONS: 135 deluxe guest rooms and executive suites, and 90 one- and two-bedroom villas and townhomes. AMENITIES: 27 holes of golf; 12 tennis courts; whirlpools and saunas; two swimming pools. RATES: From $79 daily.

Villas by the Sea Hotel *1175 North Beachview Drive, Jekyll Island, GA 31527 (800) 841-6262; In GA (800) 342-6872; (912) 635-2521.* ACCOMMODATIONS: 170 one-, two-, and three-bedroom villas. AMENITIES: Beach, swimming pol, tennis, restaurant, deli. RATES: From $44 daily.

Index of Courses

* Recommended. ** Highly recommended. **Bold face** indicates a featured course or resort. *Italics* indicate a photo.

Photo credits

Mike Klemme/Golfoto: pp. 20, 28, 52, 78-79, 96-97, 110-111, 136-137, 144, 147, 158-159.
Chris Duthie: pp. 87, 89, 94, 94-95, 108, 136, 147, 166.
Michael Tenney: pp.3, 12-13, 16-17, 18, 18-19, 21, 24-25, 26, 30, 62-63, 66-67, 72, 74-77.
Mark Brown: 34-35, 50, 143, 152, 176-177.
Sea Pines: 9, 132-133 (both by Hugh Owen).
Lake Toxaway: p. 11.
Pine Needles: pp. 38-39 (Pete Winkel), 47 (McKenzie & Dickerson), 47.
The Legacy: p. 40 (McKenzie & Dickerson).
Talamore: p. 42 (McKenzie & Dickerson).
Pinehurst Resort: pp. 42, 48, 52, 54 (all by Jim Moriarty).
Mid Pines: p. 44 (McKenzie & Dickerson).
Longleaf: p. 48 (Paul Barton).
Brandon Advertising: pp. 84-85, 86, 90-91, 100-101, 104-105, 109 (all by Mike Slear).
Kiawah Island Resort: pp. 114-115, 116, 120, 121.
Seabrook Island: p. 124.
Wild Dunes: pp. 126-127 (David Soliday).
Dunes West: pp. 130-131 (Lafayette).
Hilton Head National: pp. 138-139 (Lafayette).
LINKS: pp. 139 (Skip Meachen), 170 (Bill Cornelia).
Royal Golf & Tennis: pp. 150-151 (Lafayette).
The Cloister: pp. 165, 166 (both by Kaufman Associates).
Jekyll Island: pp. 172-173, 179 (Kaufman Associates).
Falkenberry & Certain: p. 175 (David Soliday).
Sea Palms: p. 176 (Jim Moriarty).
Bald Head Island: p. 69 (Ron Chapple)
The Emerald: p. 71 (David Uzzell)

About the author

Brett A. Borton was born and raised in Wilmington, Oh., and received a bachelor's degree in Journalism from Ohio University. The former editor of *Southern Links* and *Western Links* magazine and editor-in chief of *Golfer's Guide*, he is currently Director of Marketing for Greenwood Development. He is the author of two other books in *The Endless Fairway* series: *"The Golfer's Guide To The American Southwest,"* and *"The Golfer's Guide To California and Hawaii."* Borton lives on Hilton Head Island, SC, with his wife and son.

About the photographers

Mike Klemme, principal photographer for *The Endless Fairway* series, has photographed golf courses since 1984 and has appeared regularly in LINKS Magazine since 1988. Klemme, who lives in Enid, Oklahoma, is also principal photographer for *Grand Slam Golf,* and *World's Greatest Golf Resorts,* both published by Harry N. Abrams.

Chris Duthie is an accomplished golf course photographer and serves as Western Editor of LINKS Magazine. An avid golfer and former club champion, the University of Colorado graduate lives in Scottsdale, Arizona, with his wife Tammy.

The Endless Fairway Series

Florida and the Caribbean

by Edward J. Cherry
All the leading resorts and public golf courses in golf's #1 state, plus Puerto Rico,
The Florida Keys, Jamaica, Barbados, The Bahamas, The Dominican Republic,
Nevis, Antigua, and the Virgin Islands, plus a special section on cruise ship golf.
Lavishly illustrated with 123 photographs. $15.00

The American Southwest

by Brett A. Borton
All the leading resorts and public golf courses in Phoenix, Tucson, Las Vegas, Reno,
Lake Tahoe, and New Mexico, from the desert "target" courses to the mountain
courses of the Sierra Nevada and the Southern Rockies. 105 photographs. $15.00

California and Hawaii

by Brett A. Borton
All the leading resorts and public courses in the Western capital of golf, including
Palm Springs, San Diego, Los Angeles, Santa Barbara, the Monterey Peninsula, the
Bay Area, California's North Coast, Kauai, Lanai, Molokai, Oahu, Maui, and the
Big Island of Hawaii. 70 spectacular photographs. $15.00

The Carolinas

by Brett A. Borton. $15.00

Endless Fairway Order Form

Mail this form or call toll-free 1-800-325-6262!

__ American Southwest   __ The Carolinas

__ California & Hawaii   __ Florida and the Caribbean

Please fill in the number of books you would like to order

Name _____

Address_____

City _____ State _____ Zip _____

Please enclose $15 per book ($40 for 3), plus $3 shipping and handling per order,
and mail this form to *The Endless Fairway,* c/o LINKS magazine, P.O. Box 7628,
Hilton Head Island, SC, 29938. Or call toll-free (800) 325-6262. U.S. dollars only,
please. No C.O.D. Please allow 4 weeks for delivery.